D1734548

Eclipse IDE

Java programming, debugging, unit testing, task management and Git version control with Eclipse

Eclipse IDE: Java programming, debugging, unit testing, task management and Git version control with Eclipse

Lars Vogel

Third edition

Publication date 17.02.2013

For Jennifer, Kiran and Liam.

Thank you for the inspiration, the strength and the love you give me.

Foreword

If you ask software developers about Eclipse, most will tell you that Eclipse is an integrated development environment (IDE) for Java. Those software developers are absolutely correct: Eclipse is the most used Java IDE on the planet. With key features like code completion, content assist, incremental compilation, integrated unit testing, and more, Eclipse packs a pretty potent arsenal of tools for Java development. But there's more to Eclipse than Java development. Eclipse is a platform for tools, an integration point to provide features and functionality in a powerful and consistent manner.

Distributed version control systems are the next leap forward in that evolution, and are rapidly displacing the incumbents, with an estimated 25% of projects now using DVCS in 2011. Although SVN is still currently the most popular (as measured by lines of code under management), it has been displaced by DVCS rapidly over the last few years.

Add the C/C++ Development Tools (CDT) to your Eclipse IDE and you have an environment for building C/C++ applications. This is also true for PHP Development Tools (PDT), reporting tools, modeling, and much, much more. Eclipse can be extended to be whatever you need it to be, either by adding plug-ins via the Eclipse Marketplace, or by creating them yourself using first-class tools from the Eclipse SDK.

Eclipse is more than just technology. The Eclipse Foundation exists to foster communities of users, adopters, and developers; and an ecosystem of individuals, organizations, and companies that make a living working with open source software. The Eclipse Foundation is home to projects concerned with everything from coding and modeling, to identity management and runtimes. The best part is that just by using Eclipse, you're already part of the community. You can participate in that community at whatever level you choose: if you want to be more involved, you can open bugs, participate in project communication, contribute patches, or even start your own open source project.

But it all begins with the IDE, and that's where this book starts.

Lars Vogel has helped countless numbers of developers learn about Eclipse. As one of the most prolific writers in the Eclipse community, he sits unopposed at the top of our list of contributors of Eclipse-content tutorials; he is a frequent speaker and acknowledged expert on a variety of topics at conferences; and his professional educational offerings covering topics such as the Eclipse Rich Client Platform and Android Development are well-received. In this book, Lars uses his proven style to provide an excellent first exposure to the Eclipse Java IDE. In here, you find the foundation of knowledge that you need to springboard into more advanced topics (for which Lars is a widely-known expert) such as Android development, Google App Engine, GWT, OSGi, and more.

I look forward to having you as part of the Eclipse community.

Wayne Beaton
Director of Open Source Projects, Eclipse Foundation

Preface

1. Welcome

If you come to this book after having read other books from the *vogella* series, thank you for sticking to the series!

If you come to this book having learned about the Eclipse IDE on my website vogella.com, thank you for getting the book. I hope that this book helps you to work more efficiently.

This book demonstrates how you can develop Java applications, how you can debug them and how to write JUnit tests for your applications. It also explains how you can work with local Mylyn tasks to organize your work efficiently.

It also includes important Eclipse configuration tips which make programming with Eclipse more effective.

After finishing this book you should feel comfortable with using the Eclipse IDE for standard Java development tasks and you should be equipped to explore Eclipse further.

I hope you enjoy your learning experience.

2. Prerequisites

This book assumes no experience with Eclipse.

This book focuses on using Eclipse as a Java IDE. It does not explain the Java programming language. Even though it is possible to follow this book without programming experience in Java, the Java constructs used in this book are not explained.

If you are new to Java and Eclipse you can use this book to learn how to create and run Java programs with Eclipse and then continue to learn more about Java.

In case you picked this book to learn about the Java programming language you should start with a different reference first.

3. How this book is organized

This book gives an introduction into using the Eclipse IDE for Java development. It assumes no previous knowledge of the Eclipse IDE and can be used by a new user to learn the Eclipse IDE. Instead of presenting all possible options, this book focuses on the important parts of the Eclipse IDE, e.g. how to navigate efficiently, which settings helps you to get more productive and the like.

It also contains lots of tips which allow advanced Eclipse users to work more productive with the Eclipse IDE.

You learn how to create Java programs with Eclipse and how to run them within and outside of Eclipse. Debugging and unit testing are an important part in the daily work of a developer therefore these topics are also covered in detail.

You find lots of examples and exercises to practice.

The book also explains the usage of the Git version control system within Eclipse as Git is becoming more and more the dominate version control system.

As an add-on the book also gives a small introduction into the development of Eclipse plug-ins. This chapter might make you curious about learning more about the internals of the Eclipse IDE.

The final chapter lists helpful web resources, which should help you on your journey to learn the Eclipse IDE and the Eclipse framework.

The appendix lists useful Eclipse shortcuts which should make any Eclipse programmer more efficient in using the Eclipse IDE.

4. Errata

Every book has errors/mistakes to a certain degree. You can find a list of the known bugs on the errata page of the vogella.com website. The URL to this page is http://www.vogella.com/book/eclipseide/errata.html

In case you find errors which are not yet reported, please send an error report by email to: `<erratabooks@vogella.com>`.

Errors might be one of the following:

- Typographical errors

- Examples that do not work as described in the book

- Factual errors that are not open to interpretation

5. About the Author

Lars Vogel is the founder and CEO of the *vogella GmbH* and works as an Eclipse, Git and Android consultant, trainer and book author.

He is a regular speaker at international conferences, as for example EclipseCon, Devoxx, OOP, Droidcon and O'Reilly's Android Open and has presented at the Google Headquarters in Mountain View.

With more than one million visitors per month his website vogella.com is one of the central sources for Eclipse and Android programming information.

Lars is a nominated *Java Champion* since 2012 and a committer in the Eclipse 4 project. He also received in 2010 the *Eclipse Top Contributor Award* and in 2012 the *Eclipse Top Newcomer Evangelist Award*.

6. Shortcuts

The shortcuts listed in this book are based on Windows and Linux. Mac users must replace in most cases the Ctrl key with the Cmd key.

7. Acknowledgements

The creation of this book did not follow the typical book creation process. It started as several tutorials on my webpage.

I would especially thank Holger Voormann, Dirk Fauth, Matthias Sohn and Elias Volanakis for their feedback on the content. I'm also very grateful to Wayne Beaton for writing the foreword.

In addition I would like to thank the Eclipse Foundation for their great work and support.

I got many suggestions or corrections from countless readers of my website and I would like to express my deepest gratitude for their contributions.

Part I. Eclipse Overview

1

Eclipse overview and terminology

This chapter gives a short introduction into the Eclipse project and the Eclipse IDE.

1.1. What is Eclipse?

Most people know Eclipse as an integrated development environment (IDE) for Java. Today it is the leading development environment for Java with a market share of approximately 65%.

Eclipse is created by an Open Source community and is used in several different areas, e.g. as a development environment for Java or Android applications. Eclipse's roots go back to 2001.

The Eclipse Open Source community has over 200 Open Source projects covering different aspects of software development.

The Eclipse projects are governed by the *Eclipse Foundation*. The *Eclipse Foundation* is a non-profit, member supported corporation that hosts the Eclipse Open Source projects and helps to cultivate both an Open Source community and an ecosystem of complementary products and services.

The Eclipse IDE can be extended with additional software components. Eclipse calls these software components *plug-ins*. Several Open Source projects and companies have extended the Eclipse IDE.

It is also possible to use Eclipse as a base for creating general purpose applications. These applications are known as Eclipse Rich Client Platform (*Eclipse RCP*) applications.

1.2. Eclipse Public License

The *Eclipse Public License* (EPL) is an Open Source software license used by the *Eclipse Foundation* for its software. The EPL is designed to be business-friendly. EPL licensed programs can be used, modified, copied and distributed free of charge. The consumer of EPL-licensed software can choose to use this software in closed source programs. Only modifications in the original EPL code must also be released as EPL code.

The *Eclipse Foundation* also validates that source code contributed to Eclipse projects is free of Intellectual Property (IP) issues. This process is known as IP cleansing.

The permissive EPL and the IP cleansing effort of the *Eclipse Foundation* makes reusing the source code of Eclipse projects attractive for business companies.

2

Eclipse installation

This chapter describes how you install the Eclipse IDE.

2.1. Java requirements of Eclipse

Eclipse requires an installed Java runtime. Eclipse 4.2 requires at least Java 5 to run.

For this book you should use Java in version 6 or higher.

Java can be downloaded in two flavors, a *JRE* (Java runtime environment) and a *JDK* (Java development tools) version.

The Eclipse IDE contains its own Java compiler hence a JRE is sufficient for most tasks with Eclipse.

The *JDK* version of Java is required if you compile Java source code on the command line and for advanced development scenarios, for example if you use automatic builds or if you develop web development.

2.2. Installation of Java

Java might already be installed on your machine. You can test this by opening a console (if you are using Windows: Win+R, enter *cmd* and press Enter) and by typing in the following command:

```
java -version
```

If Java is correctly installed, you should see some information about your Java installation. If the command line returns the information that the program could not be found, you have to install Java. The central website for installing Java is the following URL:

```
http://java.com
```

If you have problems installing Java on your system, search via Google for *How to install JDK on YOUR_OS* . This should result in helpful links. Replace *YOUR_OS* with your operating system, e.g. Windows, Ubuntu, Mac OS X, etc.

2.3. Download Eclipse

The Eclipse IDE consists out of several components. The Eclipse.org website provides pre-packaged Eclipse distributions to provide downloads for typical use cases. The *Eclipse IDE for Java Developers* distribution is specifically designed for standard Java development.

Download the *Eclipse IDE for Java Developers* package from the following URL. Ensure that you download the right version for your Java version (32 bit vs. 64 bit).

```
http://www.eclipse.org/downloads
```

The following screenshot shows the Eclipse download website for a Linux system, press on the link beside the package description, e,g, *Linux 64 Bit* to start the download.

The download is a `.zip` file.

2.4. Install Eclipse

After you downloaded the `.zip` file with the Eclipse distribution you unpack it to a local directory.

Most operating systems can extract zip files in their file browser, e.g. *Windows7* with a right mouse click on the file and selecting "Extract all...".

If in doubt, search with Google for "How to unzip a file on ...", replacing "..." with your operating system.

Warning

Extract Eclipse to a directory without spaces in its path and do not use a mapped network drive (Windows). Eclipse sometimes has problems with such a setup.

After unpacking the zip file, Eclipse is ready to be used; no additional installation procedure is required.

3

Starting and configuring Eclipse

3.1. Starting Eclipse

To start Eclipse double-click on the `eclipse.exe` (Microsoft Windows) or `eclipse` (Linux / Mac) file in the directory where you unpacked Eclipse.

The system will prompt you for a *workspace*. The *workspace* is the place in which you work. See Section 4.1, "Workspace" for more details.

Select an empty directory and press the *OK* button.

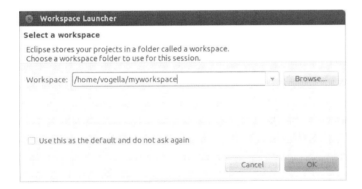

Eclipse starts and shows the *Welcome* page. Close this page by pressing the *X* beside *Welcome*.

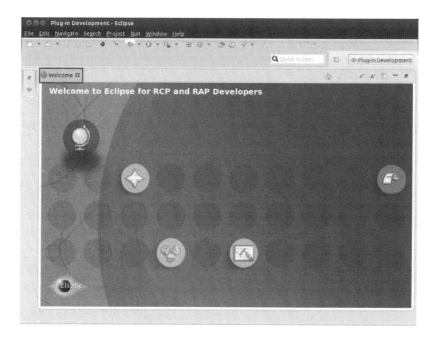

After closing the welcome screen you see a screen similar to the following screenshot.

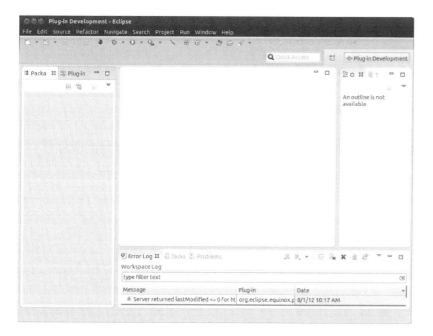

3.2. Appearance

The appearance of Eclipse can be configured. By default Eclipse ships with a few themes but you can also extend Eclipse with new themes. The appendix of this book lists popular themes.

To change the appearance, select from the menu *Window* → *Preferences* → *General* → *Appearance*.

The *Theme* selection allows you to change the appearance of your Eclipse IDE. Disabling the animations will make your Eclipse run faster.

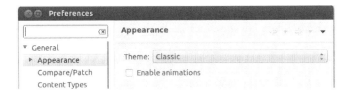

Please note that you need to restart Eclipse to apply a new theme completely.

4

Important Eclipse terminology

The following chapter explains the user interface (UI) components and some basic terminology.

4.1. Workspace

The *workspace* is the physical location (file path) you are working in. Your projects, source files, images and other artifacts can be stored and saved in your workspace. The *workspace* also contains preferences settings, plug-in specific meta data, logs etc.

You typically use different *workspaces* if you require different settings for your project or if you want to divide your projects into separate directories.

 Note

Your projects must not reside within the *workspace* directory. It is possible to refer to external resources, e.g. projects, from the *workspace*.

You can choose the workspace during startup of Eclipse or via the menu (*File → Switch Workspace → Others*) .

4.2. Eclipse projects

An Eclipse project contains source, configuration and binary files related to a certain task and groups them into buildable and reusable units. An Eclipse project can have *natures* assigned to it which describe the purpose of this project. For example the Java *nature* defines a project as Java project. Projects can have multiple natures combined to model different technical aspects.

Natures for a project are defined via the `.project` file in the project directory.

Projects in Eclipse cannot contain other projects.

4.3. Views and editors - parts

Parts are user interface components which allow you to navigate and modify data. *Parts* are typically divided into *views* and *editors*.

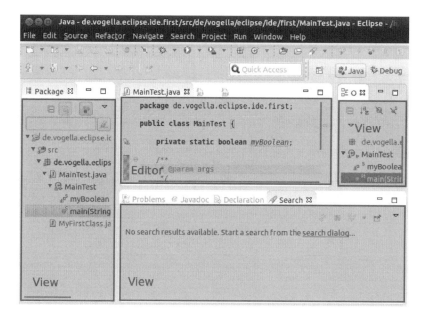

The distinction into *views* and *editors* is not based on technical differences, but on a different concept of using and arranging these *parts*.

A *view* is typically used to work on a set of data, which might be a hierarchical structure. If data is changed via the *view*, this change is typically directly applied to the underlying data structure. A *view* sometimes allows us to open an *editor* for a selected set of data.

An example for a *view* is the *Package Explorer*, which allows you to browse the files of Eclipse projects. If you change data in the *Package Explorer*, e.g. renaming a file, the file name is directly changed on the file system.

Editors are typically used to modify a single data element, e.g. a file or a data object. To apply the changes made in an editor to the data structure, the user has to explicitly save the editor content.

Editors and *views* can be freely positioned in the user interface.

For example the *Java editor* is used to modify Java source files. Changes to the source file are applied once the user selects the *Save* command. A dirty editor is marked with an asterisk.

4.4. Perspective

A *Perspective* is a visual container for a set of *parts*. The Eclipse IDE uses *perspectives* to arrange *parts* and configure the menu and the toolbar for different development tasks. Open *editors* are shared between *perspectives*, i.e. if you have an *editor* open in the *Java perspective* for a certain class and switch to the *Debug* perspective, this *editor* stays open.

You can switch *Perspectives* via the *Window → Open Perspective → Other...* menu entry.

The main perspectives used for Java development are the *Java perspective* and the *Debug perspective*.

You can change the layout and content within a *Perspective* by opening or closing *parts* and by re-arranging them.

To open a new *part* in your current *Perspective* use the *Window → Show View → Other...* menu entry. The following *Show View* dialog allows you to search for certain *parts*.

If you want to reset your current *perspective* to its default, use the *Window → Reset Perspective* menu entry.

You can save the currently selected *perspective* via *Window → Save Perspective As...*.

The *Window → Customize Perspective...* menu entry allows you to adjust the selected *perspective*. For example you can hide or show toolbar and menu entries.

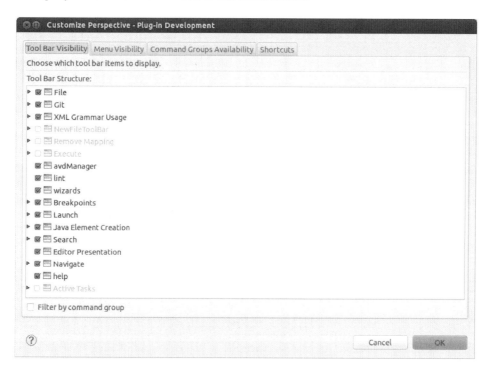

5

Java development user interface

5.1. Perspectives in Eclipse

Eclipse provides different *perspectives* for different tasks. The available *perspectives* depend on your installation.

For Java development you usually use the *Java Perspective*, but Eclipse has much more predefined *perspectives*, e.g. the *Debug perspective*.

Eclipse allows you to switch to another *perspective* via the *Window → Open Perspective → Other...* menu entry.

5.2. Resetting a perspective

A common problem is that you changed the arrangement of views and editors in your *perspective* and you want to restore Eclipse to its original state. For example you might have closed a *view*.

You can reset a *perspective* to its original state via the *Window → Reset Perspective* menu entry.

5.3. Java perspective and Package Explorer

The default *perspective* for Java development can be opened via *Window → Open Perspective → Java*.

On the left hand side, this perspective shows the *Package Explorer view*, which allows you to browse your *projects* and to select the components you want to open in an editor via a double-click.

For example to open a Java source file, open the tree under src, select the corresponding .java file and double-click it. This will open the file in the default Java *editor*.

The following picture shows the Eclipse IDE in its standard Java *perspective*. The *Package Explorer view* is on the left. In the middle you see the open *editors*. Several *editors* are stacked in the same container and you can switch between them by clicking on the corresponding tab. Via drag and drop you can move an editor to a new position in the Eclipse IDE.

To the right and below the editor area you find more *views* which were considered useful by the developer of the perspective. For example the *Javadoc view* shows the Javadoc of the selected class or method.

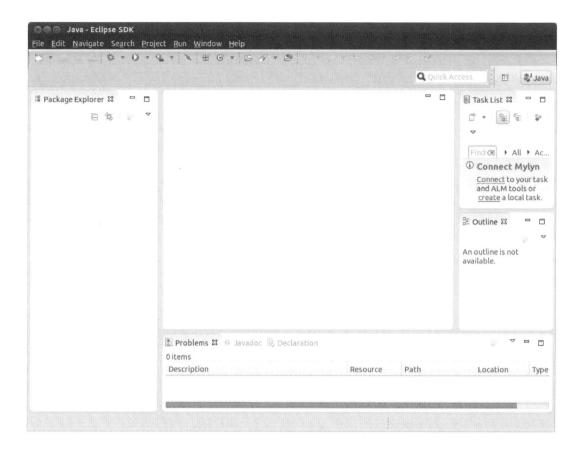

6

Java perspective overview

The following description explains the functionality of the *Java Perspective* which is the primary perspective used to develop Java applications.

6.1. Toolbar

The application toolbar contains actions which you typically perform, e.g. creating Java resources or running Java projects. It also allows you to switch between perspectives.

6.2. Useful views

The *Java perspective* contains useful *views* for working with your Java project. The following description explains the most important ones.

6.3. Package Explorer view

The *Package Explorer view* allows you to browse the structure of your projects and to open files in an *editor* via a double-click on the file.

It is also used to change the structure of your project. For example you can rename files or move files and folders via drag and drop. A right-click on a file or folder shows you the available options.

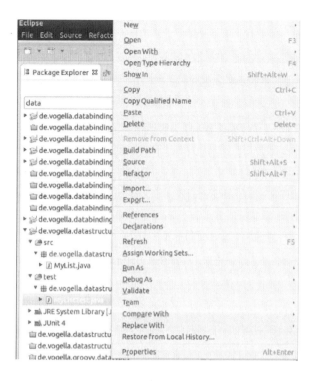

For more info on the package explorer see Section 14.1, "Package Explorer" and Section 14.4, "Link Package Explorer with editor".

6.4. Outline view

The *Outline view* shows the structure of the currently selected source file.

6.5. Problems view

The *Problems view* shows errors and warning messages. Sooner or later you will run into problems with your code or your project setup. To view the problems in your project you can use the *Problems view* which is part of the standard Java *perspective*. If this *view* is closed you can open it via *Window* → *Show View* → *Problems*.

The messages which are displayed in the *Problems view* can be configured via the drop-down menu of the *view*. For example, to display the problems from the currently selected project, select *Configure Contents* and set the Scope to *On any element in the same project*.

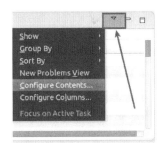

The *Problems view* also allows you to trigger a *Quick fix* via a right mouse-click on several selected messages. See Section 17.2, "Quick Fix" for details on the *Quick fix* functionality.

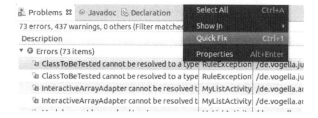

6.6. Javadoc view

The *Javadoc view* shows the documentation of the selected element in the Java *editor*.

Problems @ Javadoc ⊠ Declaration Console Terminal

⊕ **org.eclipse.swt.widgets.Button**

Instances of this class represent a selectable user interface object that issues notification when pressed and released.

Styles:
ARROW, CHECK, PUSH, RADIO, TOGGLE, FLAT, WRAP
UP, DOWN, LEFT, RIGHT, CENTER
Events:
Selection

6.7. Java editor

The Java *editor* is used to modify the Java source code. Each Java source file is opened in a separate *editor*.

```
MainTest.java    MyFirstClass.java ⊠
1 package de.vogella.eclipse.ide.first;
2
3 public class MyFirstClass {
4
5     private static final String HELLO = "Hello Eclipse!";
6
7     public static void main(String[] args) {
8         // TODO Provide user interface
9         System.out.println(HELLO);
10         int sum = 0;
11         sum = calculateSum(sum);
```

If you click in left column of the editor you can configure its properties for example that line number should be displayed.

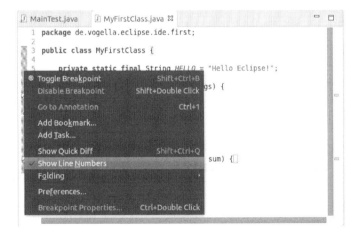

7

Exercise: Configure a perspective

7.1. Task description

A *perspective* gets adjusted for example by closing and opening *views*. Sometimes you put a perspective into an undesired state. In this exercise you practice how to configure a perspective and how to reset it.

7.2. Reset perspective

Close all *views* in the Java *perspective*.

Afterwards re-open the *Package Explorer* via *Window → Show View → Java → Package Explorer*.

Reset the Java perspective to its default configuration via the *Window → Reset Perspective* menu entry.

7.3. Save your own perspective configuration

Add the *Console* and *JUnit view* to the Java perspective.

Save this configuration as *My Java perspective* via *Window → Save Perspective As....*

8

Eclipse memory settings and start parameters

8.1. Eclipse memory settings

Your Eclipse installation contains a file called `eclipse.ini` which allows you to configure the memory parameters for the Java virtual machine which runs the Eclipse IDE. For example the $-Xmx$ parameter can be used to define how large the Java heap size can get. $-Xms$ defines the initial heap size of the Java virtual machine.

The following listing shows an example `eclipse.ini` file. The parameters after -vmargs configure the Java virtual machine. On a modern machine assigning 1024 MB or more to the Java virtual machine is good practice to run Eclipse faster.

```
-startup
plugins/org.eclipse.equinox.launcher_1.3.0.v20120522-1813.jar
--launcher.library
plugins/org.eclipse.equinox.launcher.gtk.linux.x86_64_1.1.200.v20120913-144807
-showsplash
org.eclipse.platform
--launcher.XXMaxPermSize
256m
--launcher.defaultAction
openFile
-vmargs
-Xms512m
-Xmx1024m
-XX:+UseParallelGC
-XX:PermSize=256M
-XX:MaxPermSize=512M
```

8.2. Eclipse startup parameters

Eclipse allows you to configure it via startup parameters. This requires that you start Eclipse from the command line or that you configure your launcher links to include these parameters.

The following table shows important parameters.

Table 8.1. Workspace startup parameters

Parameter	Description
-data workspace_path	Predefine the Eclipse workspace
-showLocation	Enables the display of the current workspace directory in the header of the running IDE

For example if you want to start Eclipse under Microsoft Windows using the `c:\temp` directory as *workspace* you can start Eclipse via the following command from the command line.

```
c:\eclipse.exe -data "c:\temp"
```

Depending on your platform you may have to put the path name into double quotes.

Note

You find all available runtime options in the Eclipse help [http://help.eclipse.org/] if you search for the "Eclipse runtime options" term.

Part II. Getting started with Java development in Eclipse

9

Exercise: Creating Java applications

This chapter demonstrates how to create a Java program and how to run it inside Eclipse.

9.1. Target of this exercise

The following section describes how to create a minimal Java application using Eclipse. It is tradition in the programming world to create a small program which writes "Hello World" to the console. We will adapt this tradition and will write "Hello Eclipse!" to the console.

9.2. Create project

This book uses the naming convention that the project is named the same as the top-level package in the project.

Select *File → New → Java project* from the menu. Enter `de.vogella.eclipse.ide.first` as the project name. Select the *Create separate folders for sources and class files* flag.

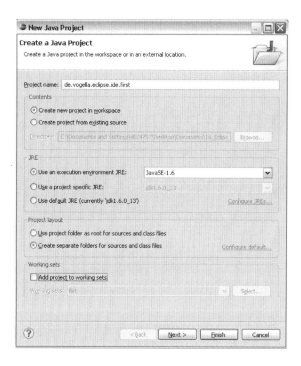

Press the *Finish* button to create the project. A new project is created and displayed as a folder. Open the `de.vogella.eclipse.ide.first` folder and explore the content of this folder.

9.3. Create package

In the following step you create a new `package`. A good convention for the project and package name is to use the same name for the top level package and the project. For example if you name your project *com.example.javaproject* you should also use `com.example.javaproject` as top level package name.

To create the `de.vogella.eclipse.ide.first` package, select the `src` folder , right-click on it and select *New → Package*.

Note

Reverse domain names should be used for packages to prevent name clashes. It is relatively unlikely that another company defines a class called `test` in the `com.vogella` package because this is the reverse URL of the vogella GmbH company.

Enter the name of your new package in the dialog and press the *Finish* button.

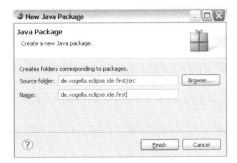

9.4. Create Java class

Create a Java class. Right-click on your package and select *New → Class*.

Enter MyFirstClass as the class name and select the *public static void main (String[ ] args)* flag.

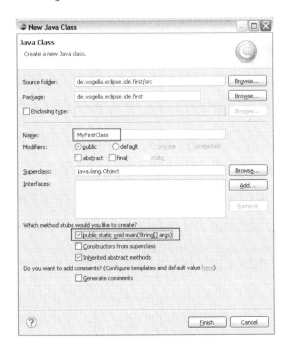

Press the *Finish* button.

This creates a new file and opens the Java *editor*. Change the class based on the following listing.

```java
package de.vogella.eclipse.ide.first;

public class MyFirstClass {

  public static void main(String[] args) {
    System.out.println("Hello Eclipse!");
  }

}
```

You could also directly create new packages via this dialog. If you enter a new package in this dialog, it is created automatically.

9.5. Run your project in Eclipse

Now run your code. Either right-click on your Java class in the *Package Explorer* or right-click in the Java class and select *Run-as → Java application*.

Eclipse will run your Java program. You should see the output in the *Console view*.

Congratulations! You created your first Java project, a package, a Java class and you ran this program inside Eclipse.

10

Exercise: Java project, packages and import statements

10.1. Create project

Create a new Java project called *com.vogella.ide.counter*

Create the following packages:

- com.vogella.ide.counter.util

- com.vogella.ide.counter.main

10.2. Create classes

Create the following Counter class in the *.util package.

```java
package com.vogella.ide.counter.util;

public class Counter {
  public int count (int x){
    // TODO check that x > 0 and <= 255
    // if not throw a new RuntimeException
    // Example for a RuntimeException:

    // throw new RuntimeException("x should be between 1 and 255");

    // TODO calculate the numbers from 1 to x
    // For example if x is 5, calculate
    // 1 + 2 + 3 + 4 + 5


    // TODO return your calculated value
    // instead of 0
    return 0;
  }
}
```

Create the following Tester class in the *.main package. This is a simple class without the usage of any unit testing framework like *JUnit*. The Eclipse editor should mark the created class with an error because the required import statements are missing.

```
package com.vogella.ide.counter.main;

public class Tester {

  public static void main(String[] args) {
    Counter counter = new Counter();
  }

}
```

Right-click in your Java editor and select *Source → Organize Imports* to add the required import statements to your Java class.

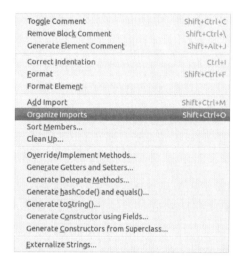

This should remove the syntax error. Finish the implementation for the `Tester` class based on the following code.

```
package com.vogella.ide.counter.main;

import com.vogella.ide.counter.util.Counter;

public class Tester {

  public static void main(String[] args) {
    Counter counter = new Counter();
    int result = counter.count(5);
    if (result == 15) {
      System.out.println("Correct");
    } else {
      System.out.println("False");
    }
    try {
      counter.count(256);
    } catch (RuntimeException e) {
      System.out.println("Works as exepected");
    }
  }

}
```

The `Counter` class had in its source code a comment starting with *TODO*. Finish the source code and calculate the correct values.

Run the `Tester` class and validate that your implementation is correct. The `Tester` class checks for an example value but the method should work for different input values.

Exercise: Run Java program outside Eclipse

This chapter demonstrates how to run a Java program outside Eclipse.

11.1. Create JAR file

To run the Java program outside of the Eclipse IDE you need to export it as a JAR file. A JAR file is the standard distribution format for Java applications.

Select your project, right-click it and select the *Export* menu entry.

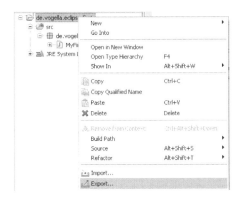

Select *JAR file* and select the *Next* button. Select your project and enter the export destination and a name for the JAR file. I named it myprogram.jar.

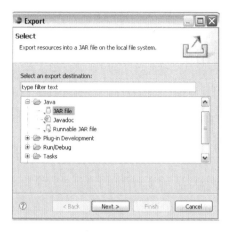

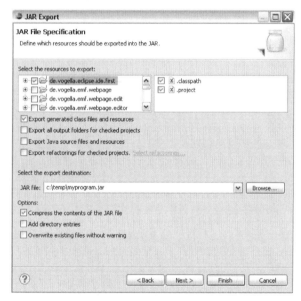

Press The *Finish* button. This creates a JAR file in your selected output directory.

11.2. Run your program outside Eclipse

Open a command shell, e.g. under Microsoft Windows select *Start* → *Run* and type cmd and press enter. This should open a console.

Switch to the directory which contains the JAR file , by typing cd path. For example if your jar is located in c:\temp use the following command.

```
cd c:\temp
```

To run this program include the JAR file into your classpath. The classpath defines which Java classes are available to the Java runtime. You can add a jar file to the classpath with the -classpath option.

```
java -classpath myprogram.jar de.vogella.eclipse.ide.first.MyFirstClass
```

Type the above command in the directory you used for the export and you see the "Hello Eclipse!" output in your command shell.

```
C:\temp>java -classpath myprogram.jar de.vogella.eclipse.ide.first.MyFirstClass
Hello Eclipse!
```

12

Exporting and importing Eclipse projects

12.1. Exporting projects

You can export and import Eclipse projects. This allows you to to share projects with other people and to import existing projects.

To export Eclipse projects, select *File → Export → General → Archive File* and select the projects you want to export.

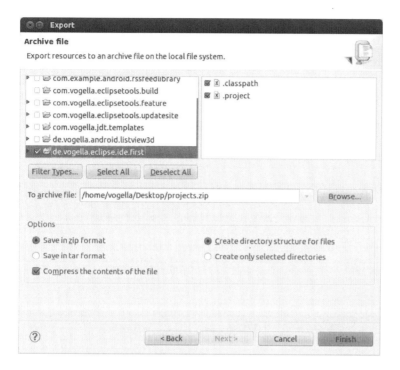

12.2. Importing projects

To import projects, select *File → Import → Existing Projects into Workspace*. You can import from an archive file, i.e. zip file or directly import the projects in case you have extracted the zip file.

13

Exercise: Export and import projects

13.1. Export project

Export your `com.vogella.ide.counter project` into a zip file.

13.2. Import project

Switch into a new workspace and import the project into your new workspace based on the zip file you exported.

Part III. Java source navigation and opening resources

14

Navigation with the Package Explorer view

14.1. Package Explorer

The primary way of navigating through your project is the *Package Explorer*. You can open nodes in the tree and open a file in an editor by double-clicking on the corresponding entry in the *Package Explorer*.

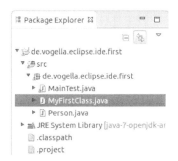

14.2. Filter resources in the Package Explorer

The drop-down menu in the *Package Explorer* allows you to filter the resources which should be displayed or hidden.

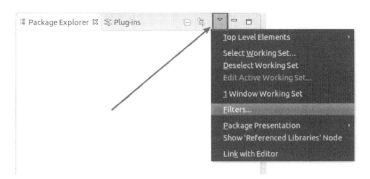

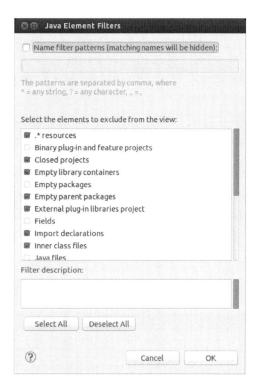

14.3. Closing and opening projects

You can close projects via right-click and by selecting the *Close Project* menu entry. Alternatively if you work on a project you can close all unrelated projects via right-click and by selecting the *Close Unrelated Projects* menu entry.

Closing projects saves memory in Eclipse and can reduce the build time. To open a closed project double-click on it, or right-click it and select *Open Project*.

Eclipse ignores closed projects, e.g. the *Problems view* does only show errors of closed projects. This typically helps to focus your attention on the project.

Tip

You can use the filter functionality for the *Package Explorer view* to hide the closed projects.

14.4. Link Package Explorer with editor

The *Package Explorer view* allows you to display the associated file from the currently selected editor. For example if you are working on the Foo.java file in the Java *editor* and switch to the Java *editor* of the Var.java file, then the corresponding file will be selected in the *Package Explorer view*.

To activate this behavior, press the *Link with Editor* button in the *Package explorer view* as depicted in the following screenshot.

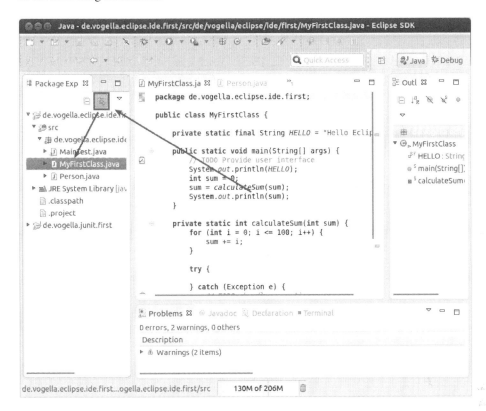

15

Navigating in the Java source code

You can also use other means than the Package Explorer to navigate your source code. The following description lists the most important ones.

15.1. Opening a class

You can navigate between the classes in your project via the *Package Explorer view* as described before. You can navigate the tree and open a file via double-click.

In addition you can open any class by positioning the cursor on the class in an editor and pressing **F3**. Alternatively, you can press **Ctrl+Shift+T**. This shows the following dialog in which you can enter the class name to open it.

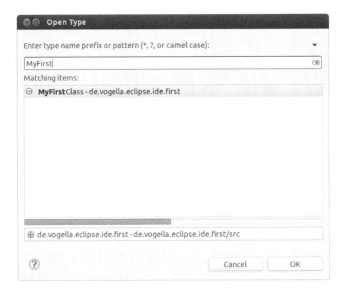

You can also search for package names. Each part of the package name must end with a . (the *dot* character) so that the *Open Type Dialog* can identify it as package.

Tip

You only need to specify part of each segment of the package name. Assume for example that you search for the *org.eclipse.swt.widgets.Button* class. To

find this class you can use the search term `org.eclipse.swt.widgets.Button`
or `o.e.s.w.Button` or `o.Button`.

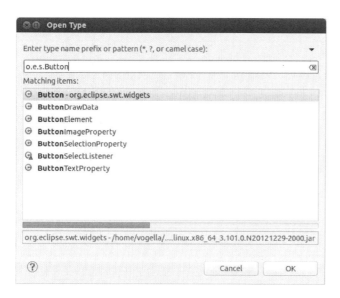

The *Open Type Dialog* also supports *camel-case* like search, e.g. it matches capital letters in the class name. For example if you would search for the `OnTouchListener` class you could use `OTL` or `OToList` as search term.

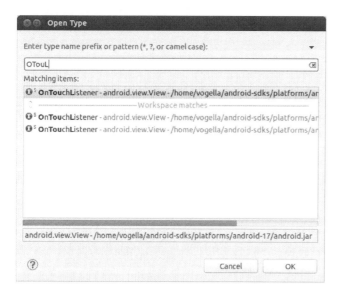

Tip

To avoid suffix matching you can add a space after the class name. For example you can type *Selection* (there is a space after selection) to match the `Selection` class but not the `SelectionListener` class. Wildcards like * are also supported.

15.2. Mouse and keyboard navigation

In lot of cases you can also use the mouse to navigate to or into an element if you press the **Ctrl** key. For example press the **Ctrl** key and (left) click with the mouse on the name of a class to jump into the class declaration.

Similar to the left mouse click combined with the **Ctrl**, you can use the **F3** key to go into a class.

15.3. Quick Outline

If you right-click in your Java editor, you can select the *Quick Outline* option which shows you an outline of your Java class with the option to filter.

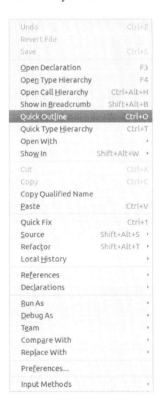

The shortcut for opening the *Quick Outline* is **Ctrl+O**. By default *Quick Outline* shows only the direct members and fields of the class. Press **Ctrl+O** again to show also the inherited members and fields.

The default look of the *Quick Outline* option is similiar to the *Quick Outline view* of the *Java perspective*.

15.4. Open Type Hierarchy

The type hierarchy of a class shows you which classes it extends and which interfaces it implements. You can use the type hierarchy to navigate to one of these elements.

To open the type hierarchy of the selected class, right-click in the editor and select *Open Type Hierarchy* (Shortcut: **F4**) or *Quick Type Hierarchy* (Shortcut: **Ctrl+T**).

15.5. Search dialog

Via the *Search → Search* menu (Shortcut: **Ctrl+H**) you can open the search dialog of Eclipse.

Use the *Java Search* tab to search for Java elements, e.g. methods.

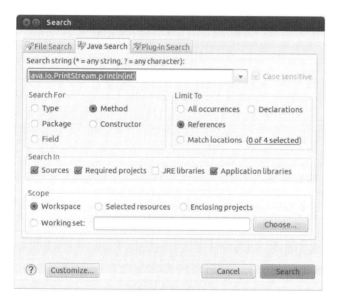

The *Search view* shows the search results for the selected scope. You can double-click on a search entry to navigate to the corresponding position in the editor. The currently selected search result is also indicated via an arrow in the left border of the editor.

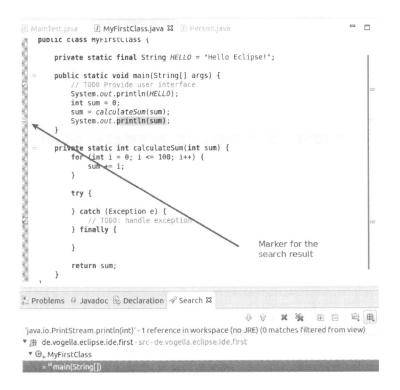

Use the *File Search* tab to search for text.

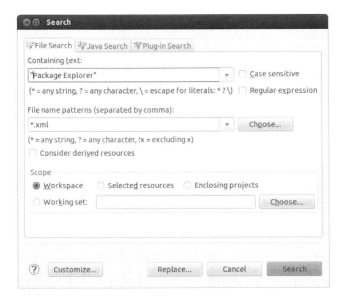

Eclipse associates file extensions with the default tab. You can customize the available search tabs via the *Customize* button in the Search dialog. Via the *Remenber the last used page* you can configure Eclipse to use your last tab as default.

Tip

The *Search view* allows you to delete search results via the **Delete** key.

15.6. Incremental find

You can use the **Ctrl+J** shortcut to activate *Incremental Find*. This allows you to search in the current active editor for a text which is displayed in the status line as depicted by the following screenshot. Repeat **Ctrl+J** in order to move to the next occurrences of the current search term.

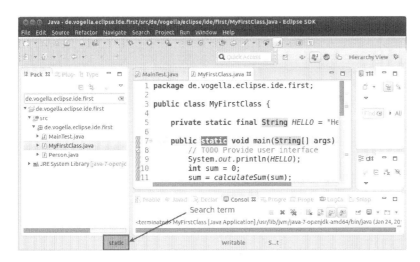

The advantage of this search is that no pop-up dialog is opened which blocks other elements in the Eclipse IDE.

15.7. Find element based on current selection

If you have selected an element in the editor you can use the **Ctrl+K** shortcut to search for the next occurrence of the selected text and **Ctrl+Shift+K** for the previous element.

15.8. Annotation navigations

You can also navigate via the annotation buttons, e.g. for jumping to the next error or warning in your source code.

By pressing the buttons you can navigate to the related annotations. You can also use the keyboard shortcut **Ctrl+.** (Ctrl plus the dot sign) for selecting the next annotation or **Ctrl+,** for selecting the previous annotation.

The following screenshot shows source code with two warnings and one error and you can navigate between the corresponding code via the annotation buttons.

```
AnnotationTestNavigation.java 

    package de.vogella.eclipse.ide.first;

    public class AnnotationTestNavigation {

        /**
         * @param args
         */
        public static void main(String[] args) {
            // Warning in Eclipse as test is not used
            boolean test = false;

            // Warning in Eclipse as s is not used
            String s = "unused";

        }

        public void testMethod() {
            // Syntax error in Eclipse because of missing
            // semicolumn
            System.out.println("test")
        }
    }
```

Which annotations are relevant for navigation can be configured via the drop-down menu of the toolbar. This selection is highlighted in the following screenshot.

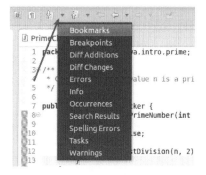

15.9. Show in Breadcrumb

You can also activate the *breadcrumb* mode for the Java editor which allows you to navigate the source code directly from the Java editor.

You can activate this mode via right-click in the editor and by selecting the *Show in Breadcrumb* entry.

This allows you to navigate the source code from the editor as depicted in the following screenshot.

MyFirstClass.java

de.vogella.eclipse.ide.first ▸ src ▸ de.vogella.eclipse.ide.first ▸ MyFirstClass ▸ main(String[]) : void

```java
package de.vogella.eclipse.ide.first;

public class MyFirstClass {
    public static void main(String[] args) {
        System.out.println("Hello Eclipse!");
    }
}
```

To hide it again, right-click on a breakcrump entry and select *Hide Breadcrumb*.

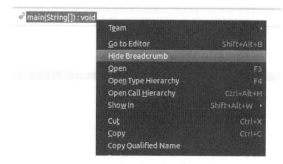

15.10. Shortcuts

There are a lot of shortcuts available for navigation. Please check the appendix of this book for these shortcuts or open *Preferences* → *General* → *Keys* to find and redefine shortcuts at runtime.

16

Opening resources

16.1. Via Package Explorer view

You can also navigate to non Java source files via the *Package Explorer view* and open a file via double-click.

16.2. Open Resource dialog

In addition to the *Package Explorer view* you can open any file in your projects via the *Open Resource* dialog which can be opened via the **Ctrl+Shift+R** shortcut. This shortcut opens a dialog in which you can enter the resource name to open it.

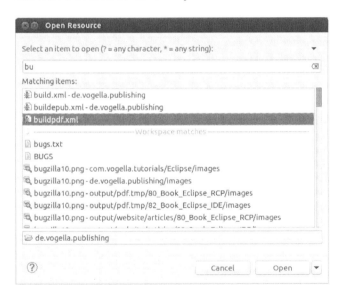

Part IV. Eclipse code generation and refactoring

17

Eclipse code generation

This chapter introduces the important concepts of *Quick Fix* and *Content Assist* which allows you to work efficiently in Eclipse.

It also shows how to use some of the code generation facilities of Eclipse.

17.1. Content assist

Content assist is a functionality in Eclipse which allows the developer to get context sensitive code completion in an editor upon user request.

It can be invoked by pressing **Ctrl+Space**

For example type `syso` in the editor of a Java source file and then press **Ctrl+Space**. This will replace `syso` with `System.out.println("")`.

If you have a reference to an object, for example the object `person` of the type `Person` and need to see its methods, type `person.` and press **Ctrl+Space**.

17.2. Quick Fix

Whenever Eclipse detects a problem, it will underline the problematic text in the editor. Select the underlined text and press **Ctrl+1** to see proposals how to solve this problem. This functionality is called *Quick Fix*.

For example type `myBoolean = true;` If myBoolean is not yet defined, Eclipse will highlight it as an error. Select the variable and press **Ctrl+1**, Eclipse will suggest creating a field or local variable.

```
package de.vogella.eclipse.ide.first;

public class MainTest {

    /**
     * @param args
     */
    public static void main(String[] args) {
        myBoolean = true;
    }
}
```

> myBoolean cannot be resolved to a variable
>
> 4 quick fixes available:
>
> ⊙ Create local variable 'myBoolean'
> ▫ Create field 'myBoolean'
> ⊙ Create parameter 'myBoolean'
> ✖ Remove assignment
>
> Press 'F2' for focus

Quick Fix is extremely powerful. For example it allows you to create new local variables and fields as well as new methods and new classes. Or it can put try-catch statements around your exceptions. It can also assign a statement to a variable and much more.

Quick Fix also gives several options for code changes on code which does not contain errors, e.g. it allows you to convert a local variable to a field.

17.3. Generating code

Eclipse has several possibilities to generate code for you. This can save significant time during development.

For example Eclipse can override methods from superclasses and generate the `toString()`, `hashcode()` and `equals()` methods. It can also generate getter and setter methods for attributes of your Java class.

You can find these options in the Source menu.

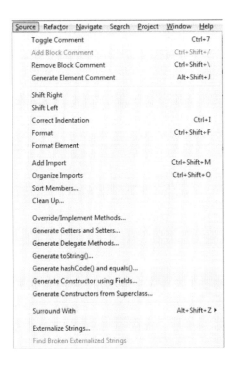

To test the source generation, create the following class in your `de.vogella.eclipse.ide.first` project.

```java
package de.vogella.eclipse.ide.first;

public class Person {
  private String firstName;
  private String lastName;

}
```

Select *Source → Generate Constructor from Fields*, mark both fields and press the *OK* button.

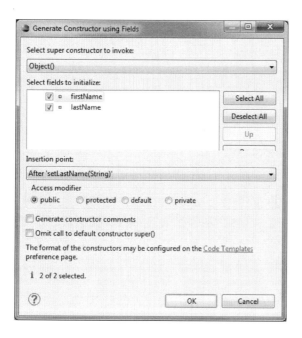

Select *Source → Generate Getter and Setter*, select again both of your fields and then the *OK* button.

Select *Source → Generate toString()*, mark again both fields and press the *OK* button.

You created the following class:

```java
package de.vogella.eclipse.ide.first;

public class Person {
  private String firstName;
  private String lastName;

  public Person(String firstName, String lastName) {
    super();
    this.firstName = firstName;
    this.lastName = lastName;
  }

  public String getFirstName() {
    return firstName;
  }

  public void setFirstName(String firstName) {
    this.firstName = firstName;
  }

  public String getLastName() {
    return lastName;
  }

  public void setLastName(String lastName) {
```

```
    this.lastName = lastName;
}

@Override
public String toString() {
    return "Person [firstName=" + firstName + ", lastName=" + lastName
        + "]";
}

}
```

Exercise: code generation and content assists

18.1. Introduction

In this exercise you practice the usage of code generation and the usage of the *Content Assists* functionality.

18.2. Create project

Create a project called `com.vogella.ide.todo`.

18.3. Create class

Create the `com.vogella.ide.todo` package and the following class.

```java
package com.vogella.ide.todo;

import java.util.Date;

public class Todo {

    private long id;
    private String summary = "";
    private String description = "";
    private boolean done = false;
    private Date dueDate;

}
```

Select *Source → Generate Constructor using Fields* to generate a constructor using all fields.

Use the *Source → Generate Getter and Setter* to create getters and setters for all fields.

The resulting class should look like the following listing.

```java
package com.vogella.ide.todo;

import java.util.Date;

public class Todo {
```

```java
  private long id;
  private String summary = "";
  private String description = "";
  private boolean done = false;
  private Date dueDate;

  public Todo(long id, String summary, String description, boolean done,
      Date dueDate) {
    this.id = id;
    this.summary = summary;
    this.description = description;
    this.done = done;
    this.dueDate = dueDate;

  }

  public long getId() {
    return id;
  }

  public void setId(long id) {
    this.id = id;
  }

  public String getSummary() {
    return summary;
  }

  public void setSummary(String summary) {
    this.summary = summary;
  }

  public String getDescription() {
    return description;
  }

  public void setDescription(String description) {
    this.description = description;
  }

  public boolean isDone() {
    return done;
  }

  public void setDone(boolean done) {
    this.done = done;
  }

  public Date getDueDate() {
    return dueDate;
  }

  public void setDueDate(Date dueDate) {
    this.dueDate = dueDate;
  }

}
```

Use Eclipse to generate a `toString()` method for the `Todo` class based on the *id* and *summary* field. This can be done via the Eclipse menu *Source → Generate toString()*.

Also use Eclipse to generate a `hashCode()` and `equals()` method based on the *id* field. This can be done via the Eclipse menu *Source → Generate hashCode() and equals()*.

18.4. Create instances

Create a new class called `TodoProvider`. Create the following static method in your `TodoProvider` class.

```
// Helper method to get a list
// of Todo objects

// Example data, change if you like
  public static List<Todo> createInitialModel() {
    ArrayList<Todo> list = new ArrayList<Todo>();
    list.add(createTodo("SWT", "Learn Widgets"));
    list.add(createTodo("JFace", "Especially Viewers!"));
    list.add(createTodo("DI", "@Inject looks interesting"));
    list.add(createTodo("OSGi", "Services"));
    list.add(createTodo("Compatibility Layer","Run Eclipse 3.x"));
    return list;
  }

  private static Todo createTodo(String summary, String description) {
    return new Todo(current++, summary, description, false, new Date());
  }
```

18.5. Write a test class

Write another `TodoProviderTest` class with a `public static void main (String[] args)` method.

In your main method call the `createInitialModel` method and validate that the returned number of items is 5.

If another number than 5 is returned, throw a `RuntimeException`. If the correct number is returned, write the String "Correct" to the *Console view*.

Use *Content assist* to create the `System.out.println()` based on `syso` for you.

```
public static void main(String[] args) {
    // More Coding....
    syso
}
```

```
public static void main(String[] args) {
    // More Coding....
    System.out.println();
}
```

19

Refactoring

This chapter covers the refactoring facilities of Eclipse which allow you to improve the structure of your source code.

19.1. Refactoring

Refactoring is the process of restructuring the code without changing its behavior. For example renaming a Java class or method is a refactoring activity.

19.2. Refactoring in Eclipse

Eclipse supports several refactoring activities, for example renaming or moving.

For example to use the *Rename* refactoring, you can right-click on your class (in the editor or Package Explorer) and select *Refactor → Rename* to rename your class. Eclipse will make sure that all calls in your Workspace to your class or method are renamed.

The following screenshot shows how to call the *Rename* refactoring for a class. The cursor is positioned on the class and the context menu is activated via a right-click on the class.

```
package de.vogella.eclipse.ide.first;

public class My
```

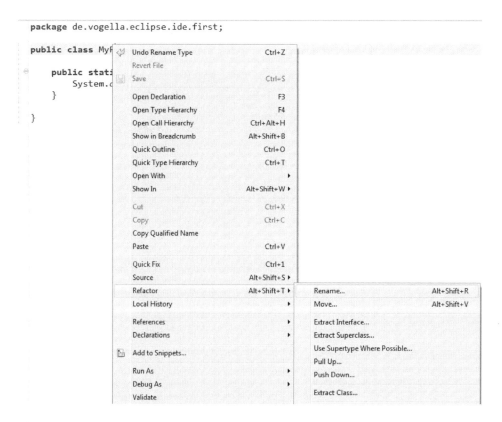

The most important refactoring are listed in the following table.

Table 19.1. Refactoring

Refactoring	Description
Rename	Rename a variable or class
Extract Method	Creates a method based on the selected code in the editor
Extract Constant	

Tip

Lots of refactorings are also available via the **Ctrl+1** shortcut (*quick fix*). Select a certain part of your code and press **Ctrl+1** to see possible refactorings which are possible at the select position.

Eclipse has many more refactorings. The available options depend on the selection in the Java editor. In most cases you should get an idea of the performed action by the naming of the refactoring operation.

20

Exercise: Refactoring

20.1. Preparation

For the next examples change the `MyFirstClass` class to the following code.

```java
package de.vogella.eclipse.ide.first;

public class MyFirstClass {

    public static void main(String[] args) {
        System.out.println("Hello Eclipse!");
        int sum = 0;
        for (int i = 1; i <= 100; i++) {
            sum += i;
        }
        System.out.println(sum);
    }
}
```

20.2. Extract method

A useful refactoring is to mark code and create a method from the selected code. To use this in this exercise, mark the coding of the "for" loop, right click on the selection and select *Refactoring* → *Extract Method*. Use *calculateSum* as the name of the new method.

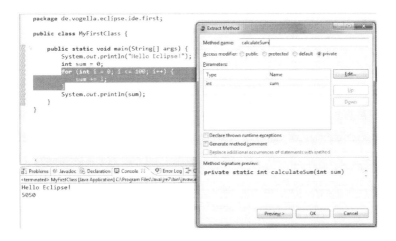

After this refactoring the class should look like the following code.

```java
package de.vogella.eclipse.ide.first;

public class MyFirstClass {

  public static void main(String[] args) {
    System.out.println("Hello Eclipse!");
    int sum = 0;
    sum = calculateSum(sum);
    System.out.println(sum);
  }

  private static int calculateSum(int sum) {
    for (int i = 1; i <= 100; i++) {
      sum += i;
    }
    return sum;
  }
}
```

20.3. Extract Constant

You can also extract strings and create constants based on the strings. Mark for this example the *Hello Eclipse!* string in your source code, right-click on it and select *Refactor → Extract Constant*. Name your new constant "HELLO".

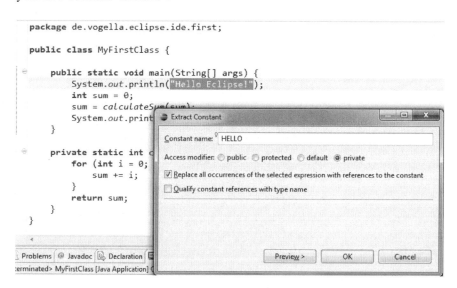

The string is now defined as a constant.

```java
package de.vogella.eclipse.ide.first;

public class MyFirstClass {
```

```java
    private static final String HELLO = "Hello Eclipse!";

    public static void main(String[] args) {
        System.out.println(HELLO);
        int sum = 0;
        sum = calculateSum(sum);
        System.out.println(sum);
    }

    private static int calculateSum(int sum) {
        for (int i = 1; i <= 100; i++) {
            sum += i;
        }
        return sum;
    }
}
```

Part V. Eclipse settings

21

Java development preference settings

Eclipse allows you to control the behavior of the IDE with preference settings. For example, you can instruct Eclipse to automatically place a semicolon you type in at the correct position or to automatically format your source code after you save a file.

21.1. Configuring the Eclipse IDE

The behavior of the Eclipse IDE can be controlled via the *Preference* settings. Select *Window* → *Preferences* to open the preference settings dialog. You can use the filter box to search for specific settings.

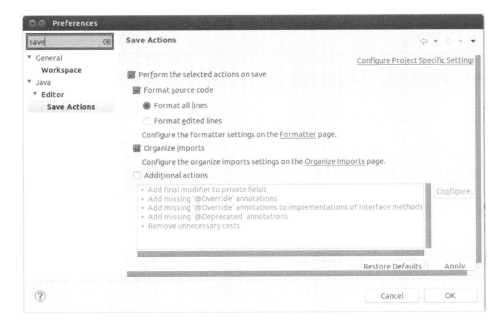

Correctly configuring Eclipse to your need can largely improve your productivity. Most of these preference settings are specific to your workspace.

21.2. Automatic placement of semicolon

Eclipse can make typing more efficient by placing semicolons at the correct position in your source code.

In the Preference setting select *Java → Editor → Typing*. In the *Automatically insert at correct position* selection enable the *Semicolons* checkbox.

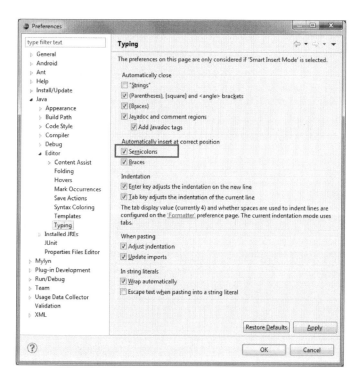

Afterwards you can type a semicolon in the middle of your code and Eclipse will position it at the end of the current statement.

21.3. Auto escape text pasted into Strings

Eclipse allows to escape text automatically if it is pasted into a String literal. For example you can copy HTML code and paste it into a String in your Java source. Eclipse would escape the text automatically for you.

Activate this setting via *Window → Preferences → Java → Editor → Typing → In string literals → Escape text when pasting into string literal*

Now you can paste text that should be escaped. The following code snippet shows an example for the resulting code if you paste HTML code containing a link into a string literal.

```
# paste <a href="tutorials.html">Tutorials</a>
```

```
# between "" of String s = ""

# results in:
String s = "<a href=\"tutorials.html\">Tutorials</a>";
```

21.4. Bracket highlighting

You can configure Eclipse to highlight the matching brackets of a code block in the source code editor.

Before the change you would not see the enclosing brackets afterwards they will be slightly highlighted. This helps to see in which block you are.

```
void foo() {
    cursor_here....
}
```

```
void foo() {
    cursor_here....
}
```

21.5. Activate Save Actions

Eclipse can format your source code and organize your import statements automatically on each save of the Java editor. This is useful as the *Save* (shortcut: **Ctrl+S**) is easy to reach.

You can find this setting under *Java → Editor → Save Actions*.

Import statements will only be automatically created, if Eclipse finds only one valid import. If Eclipse determines more than one valid import, it will not add import statements automatically. In this case you still need to right-click in your editor and select *Source* → *Organize Imports* (shortcut: **Shift+Ctrl+O**).

21.6. Filter import statements

The *Save Actions* setting automatically adds required import statements to your source code if there is only one possible import.

Alternatively or if there are several possible imports, you can use the *Organize Imports* (shortcut: **Ctrl+Shift+O**). If there are several alternatives, Eclipse suggests all available packages and the user has to select the right one.

To following shows the available packages for the `List` class in the *Organize Imports* dialog.

```
import org.eclipse.swt.SWT;
import org.eclipse.swt.widgets.Display;
import org.eclipse.s
import org.eclipse.s
import org.eclipse.s

public class FirstSW

    public static vo
        List a;
        Display disp

        Shell shell

        createUi(dis
        shell.pack()
        shell.open()
        while (!shel
            if (!dis
                disp
        }
        display.disp
    }

    private static void createUi(Display display, Shell shell) {
        Label label = new Label(shell, SWT.BORDER);
```

If you never use certain packages, for example AWT or Swing, you can exclude these packages from Eclipse via the *Window → Preferences → Java → Appearance → Type Filters* setting.

Press the *Add packages* buttons to add a specific package or the *Add* button to use wildcards. The setting in the following screenshot excludes all AWT packages from the possible imports and other Java search functionality in Eclipse.

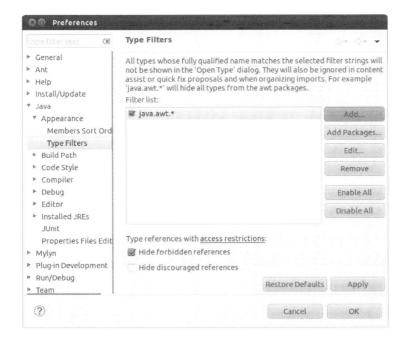

Please note that Eclipse shows (in its default configuration) only the packages that are used in the current workspace. If you want to exclude standard Java packages, you have to create at least one Java project.

21.7. Completion overwrites and insert guessed method arguments

Eclipse can override existing method calls, in case you trigger a code completion in an existing statement. Eclipse can also try to guess the correct actual parameters for a method call.

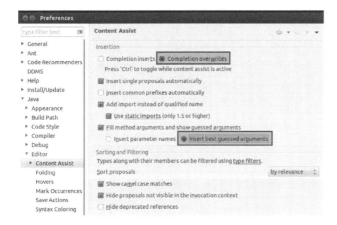

With the first setting you can override methods in the middle of a statement via the **Ctrl+Space** code assists shortcut.

```java
public class PlaygroundPart {
    public PlaygroundPart() {
        System.out.pprintln("PlaygroundPart");
    }

}
```

```
print(boolean b) : void - PrintStream
print(char c) : void - PrintStream
print(char[] s) : void - PrintStream
print(double d) : void - PrintStream
print(float f) : void - PrintStream
print(int i) : void - PrintStream
print(long l) : void - PrintStream
print(Object obj) : void - PrintStream
print(String s) : void - PrintStream
printf(String format, Object... args) : PrintStream - Pri
Press 'Ctrl+Space' to show Template Proposals
```

Without this setting you would get the following result, which results in a syntax error.

```java
public PlaygroundPart() {
    System.out.println(x)println("PlaygroundPart");

}
```

With this setting you get the following result.

```
public PlaygroundPart() {
    System.out.println("PlaygroundPart");
}
```

22

Eclipse code checks

22.1. JDT code checks

You can define how the Java compiler should react to certain common programming problems, e.g. you can define that an assignment of a variable which has no effect, e.g. x=x, causes an error in Eclipse.

22.2. Configuring the code settings

You can configure these checks in the Eclipse preferences settings via the *Java → Compiler → Errors/Warnings* entry.

22.3. Annotation based Null analysis

You can enable annotation based null checks in Eclipse via the setting highlighted in the following screenshot.

After enabling this setting you can use the @NonNull annotation on method parameters or variable definitions to indicate that these are not allowed to be NULL. You can also use the @Nullable annotation to define that a variable can be NULL.

23

More on preference settings

This chapter lists other useful Eclipse settings which are not directly related to Java development and explains how to export and import your preference settings from one workspace to another.

23.1. Launch Configuration

Eclipse allows to start an application via the *Run* button in the menu or via the **Ctrl+F11** shortcut. By default Eclipse will determine if the currently selected file is executable and try to start that. If is sometimes confusing, you can configure the Eclipse IDE to start always the last started program.

To configure that select *Window → Preferences → Run/Debug → Launching* and define that always the previous launched application should be launched.

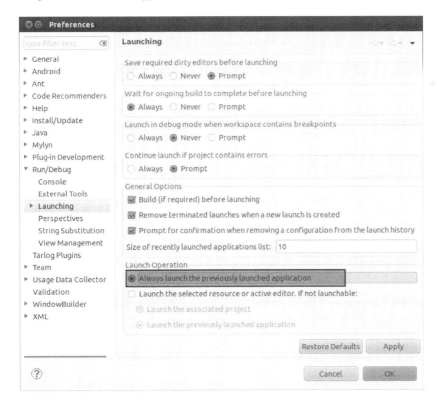

23.2. Configuring the editors for a file extension

The *Editors* which are available to open a file can be configured via *Window* → *Preferences* → *General* → *Editors* → *File Associations*.

The *Default* button in this preference dialog allows to set the default editor for a certain file extension, e.g. this is the *editor* which will be used by default if you open a new file with this extension.

The other configured *editors* can be selected, if you right-click on a file and select *Open With* In the sub-menu you see the available editors. The available editors depend on your Eclipse installation.

Eclipse will remember the last *editor* you used to open a file and use this *editor* again the next time you open the file.

23.3. Export and import preference settings

You can export your preference settings from one workspace via *File* → *Export* → *General* → *Preferences*.

Eclipse does allow to export some preference settings separately but for most of them you have to select the *Export all* flag.

Similarly you can import them again into another workspace via *File → Import → General → Preferences*.

23.4. Preference settings per project

You can also configure certain preference settings on a project basis. To do this select your project, right-click on it and select *Properties*. For example on the *Java Editor → Save Actions* you can select the *Enable project specific settings* checkbox on configure the save action on a project basis.

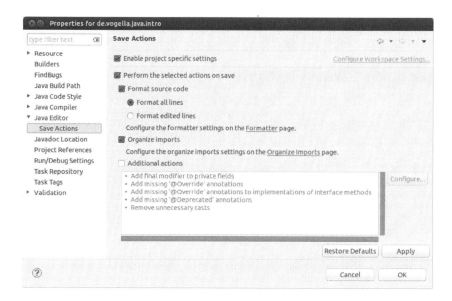

This creates a `.settings` folder which you can add to your version control system to ensure that every developer uses the same setting.

24

Exercise: Eclipse preference settings

24.1. Configuration

Certain settings in Eclipse allow you to use Eclipse more efficient. This exercise make some changes to the default Eclipse settings which typically let you develop faster.

24.2. Link Java editor with Package Explorer

If you synchronize the currently selected Java editor with the selection in the *Package Explorer view*. This gives you a clearer visibility which object you are currently editing.

Enable this by selecting the corresponding button in the *Package Explorer view*.

24.3. Java editor settings

Open the Eclipse preferences with the *Window → Preferences* menu.

Ensure that Eclipse places the semicolon and the braces automatically at the right position. Use the search box in the preferences to find this setting. A good search term is *semicolon* as depicted in the following screenshot.

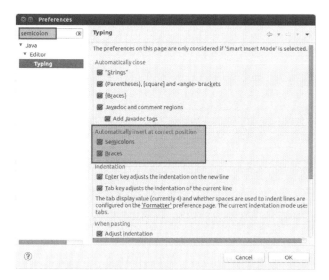

24.4. Bracket highlighting

In the Eclipse preferences activate bracket highlighting for *Enclosing brackets*.

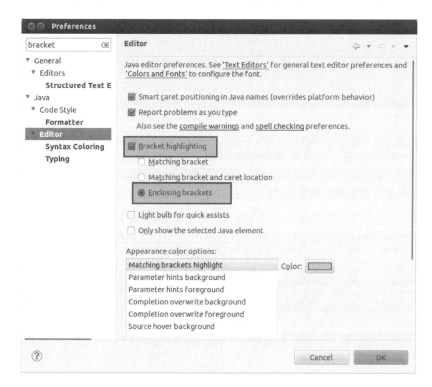

24.5. Launch configuration

Select in the Eclipse preferences select the select *Launch the previously launched application* option in the *Run/Debug → Launching* setting.

24.6. Activate Save Actions

Eclipse allows you to organize the Java imports and format your source code in the Java editor every time you save. To enable this select the *Window → Preferences → Java → Editor → Save Actions* menu and select that the source code should be formated and that the imports should be organized at every save action.

25

Setting default preference values

25.1. plug_customization.ini

You can specify default values for preferences via file which is typically called `plug_customization.ini`.

In this file you can setup default values for preference settings. For example the following will setup a default type filter for the `java.awt` and `javax.swing` package.

```
org.eclipse.jdt.ui/org.eclipse.jdt.ui.typefilter.enabled=java.awt.*;javax.swing.*;
```

You link to this file via your `eclipse.ini` file in your Eclipse installation directory.

The following example `eclipse.ini` links to the file and it assumes that you created the `plug_customization.ini` file in the Eclipse installation directory.

```
-pluginCustomization
plugin_customization.ini
-startup
plugins/org.eclipse.equinox.launcher_1.3.0.v20120522-1813.jar
--launcher.library
plugins/org.eclipse.equinox.launcher.gtk.linux.x86_64_1.1.200.v20120522-1813
-product
org.eclipse.epp.package.rcp.product
--launcher.defaultAction
openFile
-showsplash
org.eclipse.platform
--launcher.XXMaxPermSize
256m
--launcher.defaultAction
openFile
-vmargs
-Dosgi.requiredJavaVersion=1.5
-Dhelp.lucene.tokenizer=standard
-XX:MaxPermSize=256m
-Xms40m
-Xmx512m
```

25.2. Identifying preference setting values

To identify a key for a certain preference setting you can export existing preference settings via the following approach.

- start a new workspace

- change the preference

- export all preferences

- search the key in the exported file

Note

You need to remove the scope (e.g. /instance/) before copying it into the plug_customization.ini file.

25.3. Workspace Mechanics for configuring preferences settings

If you need a consistent setup of preferences for a development team or for multiple Eclipse instances, you can checkout the *Workspace Mechanics* Open Source project which is hosted under the following URL:

```
https://code.google.com/a/eclipselabs.org/p/workspacemechanic/
```

Part VI. Eclipse code templates

26

Using and configuring code templates

26.1. Templates

In Eclipse you can create templates for code snippets. This code snippets can be activated via autocomplete (**Ctrl+Space**).

For example, assume that you are frequently creating `public void name(){}` methods. You could define a template which creates the method body for you.

To create a template for this, select the menu *Window → Preferences → Java → Editor → Templates*.

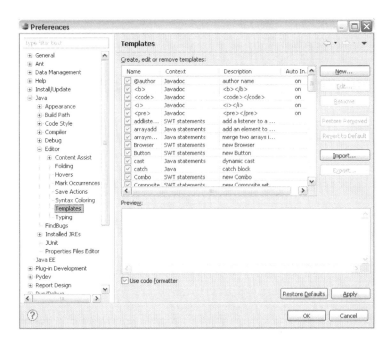

Press the *New* button. Create the template shown in the following screenshot.

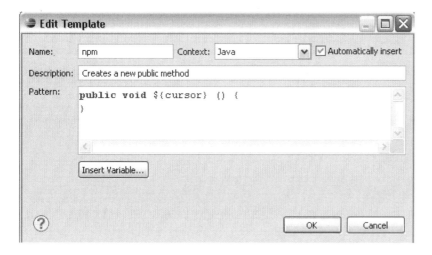

${cursor} indicates that the cursor should be placed at this position after applying the template.

In this example the name *npm* is your keyword for code completion.

Now every time you type *npm* in the Java editor and press **Ctrl+Space** the system will allow you to replace your keyword with your template.

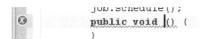

26.2. Code Formatter

Eclipse allows you also to specify the rules for the code formatter. These rules are used by Eclipse to format your source code. This allows you for example to define the settings for the usage of whitespace or for line wrapping.

You find the settings under *Window → Preferences → Java → Code Style → Formatter*.

Press the *New* button to create a new set of formatting rules or press the *Edit* button to adjust an exising profile.

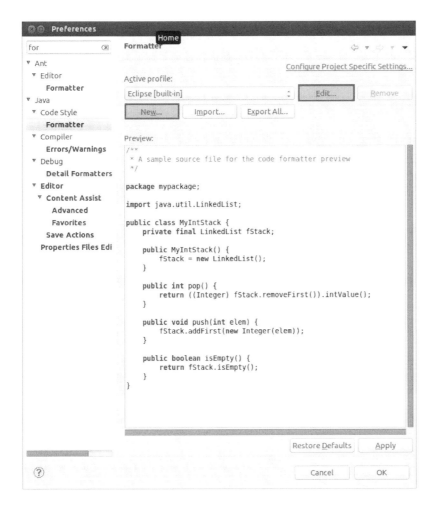

26.3. Code Templates

Eclipse can generate source code automatically. In several cases comments are added to the source code.

Select *Window → Preferences → Java → Code Style → Code Templates* to change the code generation templates.

In the code tree you have the templates. Select for example *Code → Method Body* and press the *Edit* button to edit this template and to remove the "todo" comment.

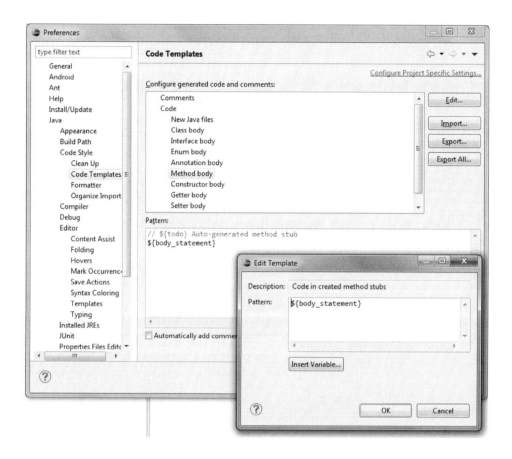

27

Exercise: Creating and using template

27.1. Create template for try/catch/finally

Create a template which creates the following block.

```
try {

} catch (Exception e) {
    // TODO: handle exception
} finally {

}
```

Place the cursor after the first bracket after the `try` statement.

27.2. Use template

Test your template in the Java editor and ensure that it works as expected.

Part VII. Local history, work organization and task management

28

Local history of files

28.1. Local history

Eclipse keeps a local history of files which have changed. Every time an editable file is saved, the Eclipse runtime updates the local history of that file and logs the changes that have been made. This local history can then be accessed and used to revert the file changes or to compare against a previous version.

28.2. Compare files based on local history

To compare the current version of a file with a local version stored by Eclipse, right-click on the file and select *Compare With → Local History...* from the context menu.

Eclipse opens the *History view*. If you double-click on an older version of the file, the *Compare view* shows the differences as depicted in the following screenshot.

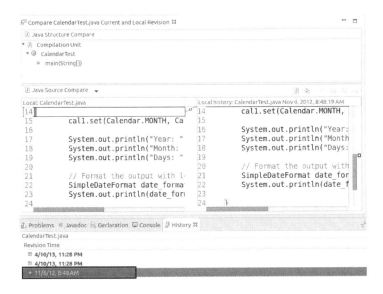

28.3. Replace files based on local history

You can replace files based on the local history. Right-click on the file and select *Replace With →
Local history...* to start this action.

Work organization with Eclipse

29.1. Working sets and tasks

The Eclipse IDE allows you to organize your project into working sets so that you can hide certain resources.

29.2. Working sets

You will create more and more projects in your development career. Therefore the data in your workspace grows and it is hard to find the right information.

You can use working sets to organize your displayed projects / data. To set up your working set select the *Package Explorer → open the drop-down menu → Select Working Set...*

Press the *New* button on the following dialog to create a working set.

On the next dialog select *Resource*, press the *Next* button and select the projects you would like to see and give it a name.

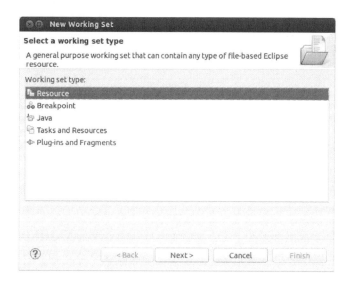

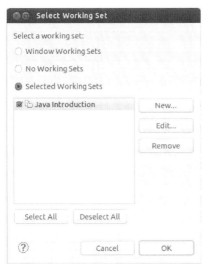

You can now filter the displayed files in the *Package Explorer* based on the created working set.

Tip

You can also use the working set to structure your projects in your workspace. For this select *Working Sets* from the context menu of the *Package Explorer view*.

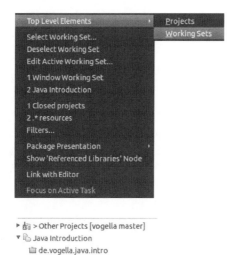

▶ 🖼 > Other Projects [vogella master]
▼ 📗 Java Introduction
    📁 de.vogella.java.intro

30

Local task management

30.1. Task management

You can place markers in the code which you can later access via the *Task view*.

You can use // TODO, // FIXME or // XXX tags in your code to add task reminders.

This indicates a task for Eclipse. You find those in the *Task view* of Eclipse. Via double-clicking on the task you can navigate to the corresponding code.

You can open this *view* via *Window → Show View → Tasks*.

For example, add a TODO to your MyFirstClass class to see it in the Tasks *view*.

```
package de.vogella.eclipse.ide.first;

public class MyFirstClass {

  private static final String HELLO = "Hello Eclipse!";

  public static void main(String[] args) {
    // TODO Provide user interface
    System.out.println(HELLO);
    int sum = 0;
    sum = calculateSum(sum);
    System.out.println(sum);
  }

  private static int calculateSum(int sum) {
    for (int i = 0; i <= 100; i++) {
      sum += i;
    }
    return sum;
  }
}
```

Close the editor for the MyFirstClass class. If you now double-click on the tasks, the Java editor opens again and the TODO comment is selected.

```
MyFirstClass.java ⊠
    public class MyFirstClass {

        private static final String HELLO = "Hello Eclipse!";

        public static void main(String[] args) {
            // TODO Provide user interface
            System.out.println(HELLO);
            int sum = 0;
            sum = calculateSum(sum);
            System.out.println(sum);
        }

        private static int calculateSum(int sum) {
```

Problems | @ Javadoc | Declaration | Console | Error Log | Call Hierarchy | Tasks ⊠

1 items

✓	!	Description	Resource	Path	Location	Type
		TODO Provide user interface	MyFirstClass.j...	/de.vogella.eclipse....	line 8	Java Task

Tip

The *Task view* shows only the tasks from the currently open projects. See Section 14.3, "Closing and opening projects".

30.2. Own tags

You can also define your own tags in the Eclipse preferences via *Window → Preferences → Java → Compiler → Task Tags*.

30.3. Mylyn

A more advanced tasks management system is available with the *Mylyn* plug-in.

Part VIII. Using Java Libraries and project dependencies

31

Using project dependencies and Java libraries

This chapter introduces the concept of Java libraries and how to use them in your Java project. You also learn how to add source and JavaDoc attachments to your library.

Eclipse can be extended with new software components. This chapter explains how you can update your Eclipse components and how to install new components.

31.1. Using project dependencies

You can define in Eclipse that a project is dependent on another project. For this select your project, right-click on it and select *Properties*.

Select *Java Build Path* and the *Projects* tab.

If you add a project to the build path of another project, you can use its classes in Eclipse.

This only works within Eclipse, outside Eclipse you need to create Java libraries for the projects and add them to the classpath of your Java application.

31.2. Defining and using Java libraries

31.2.1. What is a jar file?

A JAR file is a Java archive based on the pkzip file format. JAR files are the deployment format for Java. A JAR can contain Java classes and other resources (icons, property files, etc.) and can be executable.

You can distribute your program in a jar file or you can use existing java code via jars by putting them into your classpath.

31.2.2. Using Java libraries

If you add a JAR file to your classpath, you can use its classes in your Java application.

31.2.3. Executable jar

An executable JAR means the end-user can run the Java application without explicitly specifying the Java class which should be started. This is done via a MANIFEST.MF file which tells the JVM among other things which class contains the main() method and the classpath.

The following example shows one possible MANIFEST.MF file.

```
Manifest-Version: 1.0
Main-Class: com.vogella.example.MyApp
Class-Path:. lib/jcommon-1.0.6.jar lib/itext-1.4.6.jar
```

An empty line is required at the end of the MANIFEST.MF file.

You can create an executable JAR file via the following command.

```
jar -cvmf MANIFEST.MF app1.jar *.class
```

Eclipse provides an export wizard to create a JAR file which can be started via *File → Export → Java → JAR file*

31.3. Using jars (libraries) in Eclipse

31.3.1. Adding a Java library to the project classpath

If the libraries should be distributed with your project you can store the JAR files directly in your project.

For example you can create a new Java project de.vogella.eclipse.ide.jars. Then, create a new folder called lib by right-clicking on your project and selecting *New → Folder*.

From the menu select *File → Import → General → File System*. Select the Java library you want to import and select the lib folder as target. Alternatively, just copy and paste the jar file into the lib folder.

You can add this library to your classpath, right-click on the JAR file and select *Build Path → Add to Build Path*.

To manage your classpath, right-click on your project and select *Properties*. Under *Java Build Path → Libraries* select the *Add JARs* button.

The following example shows how the result would look like, if the junit-4.4.jar file had been added to the project.

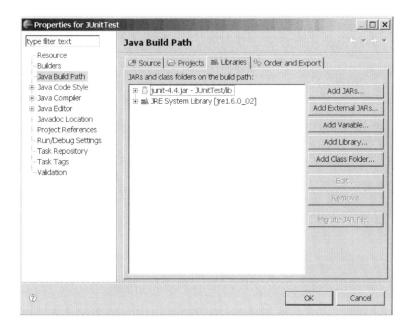

After adding it to the classpath, Eclipse allows you to use the classes contained in the JAR file in the project . Outside Eclipse you still need to configure your classpath, e.g. via the `MANIFEST.MF` file.

31.3.2. Attach source code to a Java library

You can open any class by positioning the cursor on the class in an editor and pressing **F3**. Alternatively, you can press **Ctrl+Shift+T**. This will show a dialog in which you can enter the class name to open it.

If the source code is not available, the editor will show the bytecode of that class.

This happens for example if you open a class from a the standard Java library without attaching the source code to it.

To see the source code of such a class, you can attach a source archive or source folder to a Java library. Afterwards the editor shows the source instead of the bytecode.

Attaching the source code to a library also allows you to debug this source code.

The Source Attachment dialog can be reached in the *Java Build Path* page of a project. To open this page right-click on a project and select *Properties → Java Build Path*. On the *Libraries* tab, expand the library's node, select the *Source attachment* attribute and press the *Edit* button.

In the Location path field, enter the path of an archive or a folder containing the source.

The following screenshot shows this setting for the standard Java library. If you have the Java Development Kit (JDK) installed, you should find the source in the JDK installation folder. The file is typically called `src.zip`.

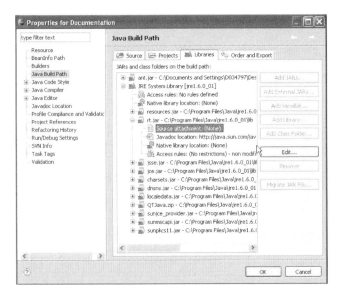

31.3.3. Add Javadoc for a JAR

It is also possible to add Javadoc to a library which you use.

Download the Javadoc of the JAR file and put it somewhere in your filesystem.

To enter the location of the Javadoc, open the *Java Build Path* via a right-click on a project and select *Properties* → *Java Build Path*. On the *Libraries* tab expand the library's node, select the `Javadoc location` attribute and press the *Edit* button.

Enter the location to the file which contains the Javadoc.

32

Using a library: User interface programming with SWT

32.1. What is SWT?

The Standard Widget Toolkit (*SWT*) is the user interface library used by Eclipse. It provides widgets, e.g. buttons and text fields, as well as layout managers. Layout managers are used to arrange the widgets according to a certain rule set.

SWT supports several platforms, e.g. Windows, Linux and Mac OS X. The design target of *SWT* is to stay closely to the operating system (OS); therefore the *SWT* API (Application Programming Interface) is very close to the native API of the OS.

As the *SWT* API is relatively low-level, programmers typically also use *JFace*.

SWT uses the native widgets of the platform whenever possible. The native widgets of the OS are accessed by the *SWT* framework via the Java Native Interface framework. The Java Native Interface (JNI) is a programming framework that enables Java code running in a Java Virtual Machine (JVM) to call, and to be called by, native applications and libraries written in other languages such as C, C ++ and assembler.

The approach of using native widgets can also be found in AWT, a standard user interface library available in Java. In comparison *SWT* provides more widgets than AWT, as AWT does not provide widgets if they are not natively available on all platforms. In case a widget is not available on one platform but on another, SWT will emulate this widget on the first and uses the native widget on the latter. For example AWT does not have table or tree widgets included, while *SWT* has.

32.2. Display and Shell

The `Display` and `Shell` classes are key components of *SWT* applications.

A `org.eclipse.swt.widgets.Shell` class represents a window.

The `org.eclipse.swt.widgets.Display` class is responsible for managing event loops, for controlling the communication between the UI thread and other threads and for managing fonts and colors. `Display` is the base for all *SWT* capabilities.

Every *SWT* application requires at least one `Display` and one or more `Shell` instances. The main `Shell` gets, as a default parameter, a `Display` as a constructor argument. Each `Shell` should be constructed with a `Display` as an input parameter.

32.3. Event loop

An event loop is needed to communicate user input events from the underlying native operating system widgets to the SWT event system.

SWT does not provide its own event loop. This means that the programmer has to explicitly start and check the event loop to update the user interface. The loop will execute the `readAndDispatch()` method which reads events from the native widgets and dispatches them to the SWT event system. The loop is executed until the main shell is closed. If this loop was left out, the application would terminate immediately.

For example the following creates an *SWT* application and creates and executes the event loop.

```
Display display = new Display();
Shell shell = new Shell(display);
shell.open();
// Create and check the event loop
while (!shell.isDisposed()) {
 if (!display.readAndDispatch())
   display.sleep();
}
display.dispose();
```

If *SWT* is used in an Eclipse Plug-in or an Eclipse RCP application, this event loop is provided by the Eclipse framework.

32.4. Using SWT in a standard Java project

It is possible to use *SWT* for stand-alone applications.

To use *SWT* in stand-alone applications, you need to have the *SWT* library available. There are several ways of doing this. You can either download the *SWT* library or create an Eclipse plug-in project and define a dependency in this project.

Download the *SWT* library from the following URL:

```
http://www.eclipse.org/swt/
```

This ZIP file contains a `swt.jar` file which you need to add to the *classpath* of your SWT project.

32.5. Event Listener

You can register listeners for specific events on SWT controls, e.g. a `ModifyListener` to listen to changes in a `Text` widget or a `SelectionLister` for selection (click) events on a `Button` widget.

```
// define PUSH Button
// for a checkbox button use SWT.CHECK stylebit

Button button = new Button(shell, SWT.PUSH);
button.addSelectionListener(new SelectionAdapter() {
    @Override
    public void widgetSelected(SelectionEvent e) {
        // Handle the selection event
        System.out.println("Called!");
    }
});
```

ModifyListener, FocusListener and SelectionListener are examples for these listener interfaces.

Eclipse usually provides empty default implementations for these interfaces. These follow the naming convention: *Name Listener* → *Name Adapter*.

For example SelectionListener has the abstract class SelectionAdapter which pre-implements the methods of SelectionListener. This allows you to use SelectionAdapter as base for an anonymous class where only one of the two declared methods are needed.

If you want to add a listener to the whole application you can use the Display class. For example to add a global mouse listener use addFilter(SWT.MouseMove, listener).

33

Exercises: Using the SWT library

33.1. Exercise: Create Java project

Create a new Java project called *com.examle.swt.widgets*. Create a new `lib` folder in your project.

Download the SWT library from the following URL and extract the archive. Ensure that you download the correct version for your Java and OS version. If you use a 32 bit Java version you need also to use the 32 bit version of SWT. Use the *more* link to find the correct version (32 bit vs. 64 bit).

```
http://www.eclipse.org/swt
```

Copy the `swt.jar` library and the `src.zip` file to the `lib` folder in your project.

Add the library to the classpath of the project. Attach the `src.zip` source zip file to the library. Use the *Open Type* dialog to open the `Shell` class. If everything has been done correctly you see the source code of the `Shell` class.

33.2. Exercise: Create a simple SWT program

Continue to use the `com.examle.swt.widgets` project.

Create the following class for a simple *SWT* application.

```
package com.example.swt.widgets;

import org.eclipse.swt.widgets.Display;
import org.eclipse.swt.widgets.Shell;

public class FirstSWTApplication {

    public static void main(String[] args) {
        Display display = new Display();

        Shell shell = new Shell(display);

        // Layout manager handle the layout
        // of the widgets in the container
        shell.setLayout(new FillLayout());

        //TODO add some widgets to the Shell
        shell.open();
        while (!shell.isDisposed()) {
            if (!display.readAndDispatch())
                display.sleep();
        }
        display.dispose();
    }
}
```

To start your application, right-click on your Java class, and select *Run-As → Java Application*. You will receive an empty window (`Shell`).

Change the TODO in the code to the following. Make sure you use `org.eclipse.swt` and not `java.awt` when adding the missing imports.

```
// Shell can be used as container
Label label = new Label(shell, SWT.BORDER);
label.setText("This is a label:");
label.setToolTipText("This is the tooltip of this label");

Text text = new Text(shell, SWT.NONE);
text.setText("This is the text in the text widget");
text.setBackground(display.getSystemColor(SWT.COLOR_BLACK));
text.setForeground(display.getSystemColor(SWT.COLOR_WHITE));

// set widgets size to their preferred size
text.pack();
label.pack();
```

If you now start the application you will get a `Shell` with two `Widgets` included.

33.3. Exercise: SWT Button

Add a Button widget to your application and assign a SelectionListener to it. If the button is pressed, write "Called!" to the console.

```java
// define PUSH Button
// for a checkbox button use SWT.CHECK stylebit

Button button = new Button(shell, SWT.PUSH);
button.addSelectionListener(new SelectionAdapter() {
    @Override
    public void widgetSelected(SelectionEvent e) {
        // Handle the selection event
        System.out.println("Called!");
    }
});
```

Part IX. Exercises: Working with Java in Eclipse

34
Overview

The following chapters help you to practice the usage of the Eclipse IDE for creating projects, packages and classes. As a side effect you get also a refresher about the Java IO, networking and the collections API.

35

Collections

35.1. Java Collections

A Java *collection* is a data structure which contains and processes a set of data. The data stored in the collection is encapsulated and the access to the data is only possible via predefined methods.

For example if your application saves data in an object of type `People`, you can store several `People` objects in a collection.

While arrays are of a fixed size, collections have a dynamic size, e.g. a collection can contain a flexible number of objects.

Typical collections are: stacks, queues, deques, lists and trees.

As of Java 5 collections should get parameterized with an object declaration to enable the compiler to check if objects which are added to the collection have the correct type.

The following code shows an example how to create a Collection of type `List`.

`List` is only an interface, a common implementation is the `ArrayList` class.

```
package collections;

import java.util.ArrayList;

public class MyArrayList {

    public static void main(String[] args) {

        // Declare the List concreate type is ArrayList
        List<String> var = new ArrayList<String>();

        // Add a few Strings to it
        var.add("Lars");
        var.add("Tom");

        // Loop over it and print the result to the console
        for (String s : var) {
            System.out.println(s);
        }
    }
}
```

The `java.util.Collections` class provides useful functionalities for working with collections.

Table 35.1. Collections

Method	Description
Collections.copy(list, list)	Copy a collection to another
Collections.reverse(list)	Reverse the order of the list
Collections.shuffle(list)	Shuffle the list
Collections.sort(list)	Sort the list

35.2. Exercise: Use Java Collections

Create a new Java project called `com.vogella.java.collections`. Also add a package with the same name.

Create a Java class called *Server* with one String attribute called *url*.

```
package com.vogella.java.collections;

public class Server {
    private String url;
}
```

Create getter and setter methods for this attribute using code generation capabilities of Eclipse. For this select *Source → Generate Getters and Setters* from the Eclipse menu.

Create via Eclipse a constructor which gets a url as parameter. For this select *Source → Generate Constructor using Fields...* from the Eclipse menu.

Type *main* in the class body and use code completion (**Ctrl+Space**) to generate a `main` method.

```
 1  package com.vogella.java.collections;
 2
 3  public class Server {
 4      private String url;
 5
 6      public Server(String url) {
 7          this.url = url;
 8      }
 9
10      public String getUrl() {
11          return url;
12      }
13
14      public void setUrl(String url) {
15          this.url = url;
16      }
17
18      main
19  }
20
```

main - main method   public static void m

                                             }

In your main method create a `List` of type `ArrayList` and add 3 objects of type `Server` objects to this list.

```java
public static void main(String[] args) {
    List<Server> list = new ArrayList<Server>();
    list.add(new Server("http://www.vogella.com"));
    list.add(new Server("http://www.google.com"));
    list.add(new Server("http://www.heise.de"));
}
```

Use code completion to create a *foreach* loop and write the `toString` method to the console. Use code completion based on `syso` for that.

Run your program.

Use Eclipse to create a `toString` method based on the *url* parameter and re-run your program again.

36

Input / Output

36.1. Overview

Java provides a standard way of reading from and writing to files. The `java.io` package contains classes which can be used to read and write files and other sources.

Java will read all input as a stream of bytes. The `InputStream` class is the superclass of all classes representing an input stream of bytes.

Classes from the `java.io` package can be chained, e.g. certain classes handle the reading and writing of an input stream of bytes while others provide a higher level of abstraction, e.g. to read a line of a file.

In general the classes in this package can be divided into the following classes:

- Connection Streams: represent connections to destinations and sources such as files or network sockets. Usually low-level.

- Chain Streams: work only if chained to another stream. Usually higher level protocol, for example they provide the functionality to read a full line of a text file.

You can access files relative to the current execution directory of your Java program. To print the current directory in which your Java program is running, you can use the following statement.

```
System.out.println(System.getProperty("user.dir"));
```

36.2. File Access Examples

To read a text file you can use the following method:

```
public String readTextFile(String fileName) {

  String returnValue = "";
  FileReader file = null;

  try {
    file = new FileReader(fileName);
    BufferedReader reader = new BufferedReader(file);
    String line = "";
    while ((line = reader.readLine()) != null) {
```

```
      returnValue += line + "\n";
    }
  } catch (Exception e) {
      throw new RuntimeException(e);
  } finally {
    if (file != null) {
      try {
        file.close();
      } catch (IOException e) {
        // Ignore issues during closing
      }
    }
  }
  return returnValue;
}
```

To write a file you can use the following method:

```
public void writeTextFile(String fileName, String s) {
    FileWriter output = null;
    try {
        output = new FileWriter(fileName);
        BufferedWriter writer = new BufferedWriter(output);
        writer.write(s);
    } catch (Exception e) {
        throw new RuntimeException(e);
    } finally {
        if (output != null) {
          try {
            output.close();
          } catch (IOException e) {
            // Ignore issues during closing
          }
        }
    }

  }
```

37

Network access

37.1. Java and HTTP access

Java provides API's to access resources over the network, for example to read webpages. The main classes to access the Internet are the `java.net.URL` class and the `java.net.HttpURLConnection` class.

The URL class can be used to define a pointer to a web resource while the `HttpURLConnection` class can be used to access a web resource.

`HttpURLConnection` allows you to create an `InputStream`.

Once you have accessed an `InputStream` you can read it similarly to an `InputStream` from a local file.

37.2. Example: Read web page via Java

Create a Java project called *de.vogella.web.html*. The following code will read an HTML page from a URL and write the result to the console.

```java
package de.vogella.web.html;

import java.io.BufferedReader;
import java.io.IOException;
import java.io.InputStreamReader;
import java.net.URL;

public class ReadWebPage {
  public static void main(String[] args) {
    String urlText = "http://www.vogella.com";
    BufferedReader in = null;
    try {
      URL url = new URL(urlText);
      in = new BufferedReader(new InputStreamReader(url.openStream()));

      String inputLine;
      while ((inputLine = in.readLine()) != null) {
        System.out.println(inputLine);
      }
    } catch (Exception e) {
      e.printStackTrace();
    } finally {
```

```java
        if (in != null) {
          try {
            in.close();
          } catch (IOException e) {
            e.printStackTrace();
          }
        }
      }
    }
  }
}
```

38

Java Annotations and Java Reflection

38.1. Annotations in Java

Annotations provide data about a class that is not part of the programming logic itself. They have no direct effect on the code they annotate. Other components can use this information. For example the @Override annotation is used by the Java compiler to check if the annotated method really overrides a method of an interface or the extended class.

Annotations can be preserved at runtime (RetentionPolicy.RUNTIME) or are only available at development time (RetentionPolicy.SOURCE).

38.2. Defining own annotations

The Java programming language allows you to define your custom annotations.

Annotations are defined via the @interface annotation before the class name. Via @Retention you define if the annotation should be retained at runtime or not. The @Target annotation lets you define where this annotation can be used, e.g. the class, fields, methods, etc.

A typical annotation definition would look like the following.

```
@Retention(RetentionPolicy.RUNTIME)
@Target(ElementType.METHOD)
public @interface InstallerMethod {
}
```

You can also define that your annotation is a qualifier for the @Inject annotation.

```
@javax.inject.Qualifier
@Documented
@Target({ElementType.FIELD, ElementType.PARAMETER})
@Retention(RetentionPolicy.RUNTIME)
public @interface Checker {

}
```

38.3. Using your annotation via Java reflection

To process your annotation you could write your own annotation processor. Typically you use Java reflection for this. Java reflection allows you to analyze a Java class and use the information contained in this class at runtime.

38.4. Exercise: Define and analyze your own annotation

Create a new Java project called *com.vogella.annotations*.

Create the following two classes. The first class defines an annotation and the second class uses this to mark certain methods.

```java
package com.vogella.annotations;

import java.lang.annotation.ElementType;
import java.lang.annotation.Retention;
import java.lang.annotation.RetentionPolicy;
import java.lang.annotation.Target;

@Target(value = ElementType.METHOD)
@Retention(value = RetentionPolicy.RUNTIME)
public @interface CanRun {

}
```

```java
package com.vogella.annotations;

import java.lang.reflect.Method;

public class AnnotationRunner {

    public void method1() {
        System.out.println("method1");
    }

    @CanRun
    public void method2() {
        System.out.println("method2");
    }

    @CanRun
    public void method3() {
        System.out.println("method3");
    }

    public void method4() {
        System.out.println("method4");
    }

    public void method5() {
        System.out.println("method5");
    }
}
```

Afterwards create the following test class. The main method of this class analyzes the annotations and calls the corresponding methods.

```java
package com.vogella.annotations;

import java.lang.reflect.Method;

public class MyTest {

    public static void main(String[] args) {

        AnnotationRunner runner = new AnnotationRunner();
        Method[] methods = runner.getClass().getMethods();

        for (Method method : methods) {
            CanRun annos = method.getAnnotation(CanRun.class);
            if (annos != null) {
                try {
                    method.invoke(runner);
                } catch (Exception e) {
                    e.printStackTrace();
                }
            }
        }
    }
}
```

39

Observer / Listener pattern in Java

39.1. Definition

The *observer* pattern defines a one-to-many dependency between objects so that when one object changes state, all of its dependents are notified and updated automatically.

The object which is being watched is called the *subject*. The objects which are watching the state changes are called *observers* or *listeners*.

39.2. Example

The observer pattern is very common in Java. For example you can define a listener for a button in a user interface. If the button is selected the listener is notified and performs a certain action.

But the observer pattern is not limited to single user interface components. For example you could have a part A in your application which displays the current temperature.

Another part B displays a green light if the temperature is above 20 degree celsius. To react to changes in the temperature part B registers itself as a listener to Part A.

If the temperature in part A is changed, an event is triggered. This event is sent to all registered listeners, as for example part B. Part B receives the changed data and can adjust its display.

The following example code shows such a listener implementation for a button.

```
Button button =  new Button(shell, SWT.PUSH);
button.addSelectionListener(new SelectionAdapter() {
  @Override
  public void widgetSelected(SelectionEvent e) {
    // Handle the selection event
    System.out.println("Called!");
  }
});
```

39.3. Code example

In the following example the observer is watching changes in a List of People objects. For this example create a new Java project called *com.vogella.java.designpattern.observer* and the following classes.

```java
package com.vogella.java.designpattern.observer;

import java.beans.PropertyChangeEvent;
import java.beans.PropertyChangeListener;
import java.util.ArrayList;
import java.util.List;

public class MyModel {

    private List<Person> persons = new ArrayList<Person>();
    private List<PropertyChangeListener> listeners =
            new ArrayList<PropertyChangeListener>();

    public class Person {

        private String firstName;

        private String lastName;

        public Person(String firstName, String lastName) {
            this.firstName = firstName;
            this.lastName = lastName;
        }

        public String getFirstName() {

            return firstName;
        }

        public void setFirstName(String firstName) {
            notifyListeners(this, "firstName",
                    firstName,
                    this.firstName = firstName);

        }

        public String getLastName() {
            return lastName;
        }

        public void setLastName(String lastName) {
            notifyListeners(this, "lastName",
                    lastName,
                    this.lastName = lastName);
        }
    }

    public List<Person> getPersons() {
        return persons;
    }

    public MyModel() {
        // Just for testing we hard-code the persons here:
        persons.add(new Person("Lars", "Vogel"));
        persons.add(new Person("Jim", "Knopf"));
    }

    private void notifyListeners(Object object,
            String property, String oldValue, String newValue) {
```

```
        for (PropertyChangeListener name : listeners) {
            name.propertyChange(new PropertyChangeEvent(this,
                        "firstName",
                        oldValue,
                        newValue));
        }
    }

    public void addChangeListener(PropertyChangeListener newListener) {
        listeners.add(newListener);
    }

}
```

```
package com.vogella.java.designpattern.observer;

import java.beans.PropertyChangeEvent;
import java.beans.PropertyChangeListener;

public class MyObserver implements PropertyChangeListener {
    public MyObserver(MyModel model) {
        model.addChangeListener(this);
    }

    @Override
    public void propertyChange(PropertyChangeEvent event) {
        System.out.println("Changed property: " + event.getPropertyName() + " old:"
                + event.getOldValue() + " new: " + event.getNewValue());
    }
}
```

```
package com.vogella.java.designpattern.observer;

import com.vogella.java.designpattern.observer.MyModel.Person;

public class Main {

  public static void main(String[] args) {
    MyModel model = new MyModel();
    MyObserver observer = new MyObserver(model);
    // We change the last name of the person, observer will get notified
    for (Person person : model.getPersons()) {
        person.setLastName(person.getLastName() + "1");
    }
    // We change the  name of the person, observer will get notified
    for (Person person : model.getPersons()) {
        person.setFirstName(person.getFirstName() + "1");
    }
  }
}
```

39.4. Evaluation

The observer pattern allows for the *Open Closed* principle. This principle states that a class should be open for extensions without the need to change the class.

Using the observer pattern a *subject* can register an unlimited number of observers. If a new listener wants to register with the subject, no code change in the subject is necessary.

Using the listener pattern decouples the subject from its observers. Only the observers have direct knowledge about the subject.

Part X. Updating Eclipse and installing components

40

Installing and updating

40.1. Eclipse update manager

Eclipse contains a software component called *Update Manager* which allows you to install and update software components. Installable software components are called `features` and consist of `plug-ins`.

These features are contained in so-called *update sites* or *software sites*. A *update site* can be for example a directory on a webserver which contains installable software components and additional configuration files.

These configuration files provide aggregated information about these software components. If Eclipse checks which software components are available on this *update site* it only needs to download and parse these configuration files to know the content of this *update site*.

40.2. Performing an update and install new features

 Warning

If you are behind a network proxy you have to configure your proxy via the *Window →
Preferences → General → Network Connection* preference setting otherwise Eclipse may
not able to reach the update sites.

To update your Eclipse installation, select *Help → Check for Updates*. The system searches for updates for the already installed software components. If it finds updated components, it will ask you to approve the update.

To install a new functionality, select *Help → Install New Software*.

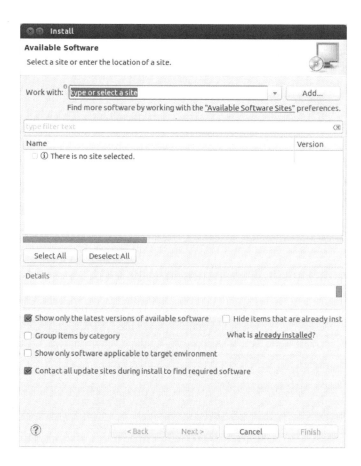

From the *Work with* list, select or enter an URL from which you would like to install new software components. Entering a new URL adds this URL automatically to the list of available update sites.

To explicitly add a new update site, press the *Add* button and enter the new URL as well as a name for the new update site.

The following update sites contain the official Eclipse components.

```
# Eclipse 4.3 (Kepler release)
http://download.eclipse.org/releases/kepler

#Eclipse 4.2 (Juno release)
http://download.eclipse.org/releases/juno
```

If you select a valid update site, Eclipse allows you to install the available components. Check the components which you want to install.

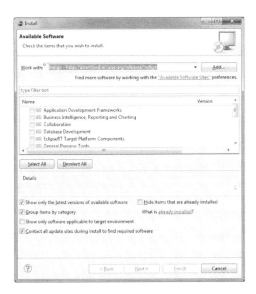

To install certain components you have to uncheck the *Group items by category* checkbox because not all available plug-ins are categorized. If they are not categorized, they will not be displayed, unless the grouping is disabled.

40.3. See the installed components

To see which components are installed use *About Eclipse → Installation Details*.

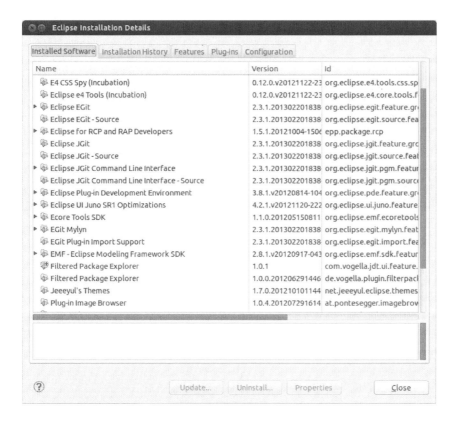

40.4. Uninstalling components

If you select *Help* → *About* and then the *Installation Details* button, you can uninstall components from your Eclipse IDE.

40.5. Restarting Eclipse

After an update or an installation of a new software component you should restart Eclipse to make sure that the changes are applied.

40.6. Eclipse Marketplace

Eclipse also contains a client which allows installing software components from the Eclipse *Marketplace client*. The advantage of this client is that you can search for components, discover popular extensions and see descriptions and ratings.

Compared to the update manager you do not have to know the URL for the *software site* which contains the installable software components.

Not all Eclipse distributions contain the *Marketplace client* by default. You may need to install the *Marketplace client* software component into Eclipse before you can use it. The following screenshot shows how to install it from one of the official Eclipse update sites.

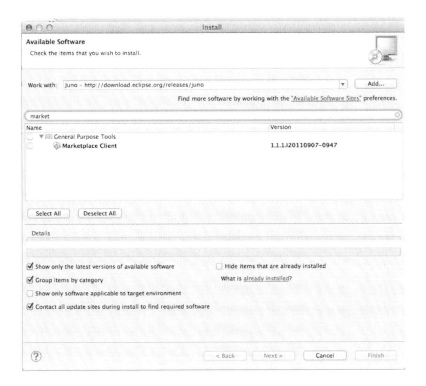

To open the Eclipse Marketplace select *Help → Eclipse Marketplace*.

You can use the *Find* box to search for components. Pressing the *Install* button starts the installation process.

41

Advanced options for updating Eclipse

41.1. Manual installation of plug-ins (dropins folder)

Eclipse plug-ins are distributed as `jar` files. If you want to use an Eclipse plug-in directly or do not know the *update site* for it, you can place it in the `dropins` folder of your Eclipse installation directory. Eclipse monitors this directory and during a (re-)start of your IDE, the Eclipse update manager installs and removes plug-in based on the files contained in this directory.

You should not modify the content of the Eclipse `plugins` directory directly. If you want to install plug-ins put them into the `dropins` folder, if you want to remove it delete the JAR from this folder.

Plug-ins are typically distributed as `jar` files. To add a plug-in to your Eclipse installation, put the plug-in .jar file into the Eclipse `dropins` folder and restart Eclipse. Eclipse should detect the new plug-in and install it for you.

If you remove plug-ins from the `dropins` folder and restart Eclipse these plug-ins are automatically removed from your Eclipse installation.

41.2. Exporting and importing the installed components

Eclipse allows you to export a file which describes the installed Eclipse components. During the export the user can select which components should be included into this description file.

Other users can import this description file into their Eclipse installation and install the components based on this file.

This way Eclipse installation can be kept in sync with each other.

To export a description file, select *File → Export → Install → Installed Software Items to File* and select the components which should be included into your description file.

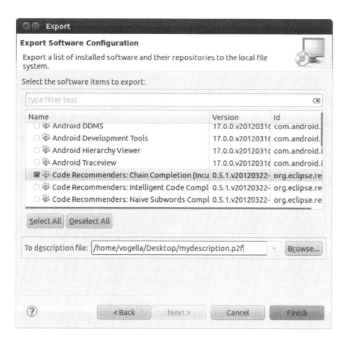

To install the described components in another Eclipse installation, open the exported file with *File →*
Import → Install → Install Software Items from File and follow the wizard. The wizard allows you to
specify the components which should be installed.

41.3. Installing features via the command line

The Eclipse update manager has a component called *director* which allows you to install new features
via the command line.

For example the following command will install the components EGit, Mylyn and EMF into an Eclipse
instance. You need to start this command in the command line and it assumes that you are in a directory
which contains your Eclipse installation in a folder called `eclipse`.

```
eclipse/eclipse \
-application org.eclipse.equinox.p2.director \
-noSplash \
-repository \
http://download.eclipse.org/releases/kepler \
-installIUs \
org.eclipse.egit.feature.group,\
org.eclipse.jgit.feature.group,\
org.eclipse.emf.sdk.feature.group,\
org.eclipse.mylyn_feature.feature.group,\
org.eclipse.wst.xml_ui.feature.feature.group,\
org.eclipse.mylyn.java_feature.feature.group,\
org.eclipse.mylyn.pde_feature.feature.group
```

The feature names which you need for this operation can be seen on the second page of the standard installation dialog of the Eclipse update manager.

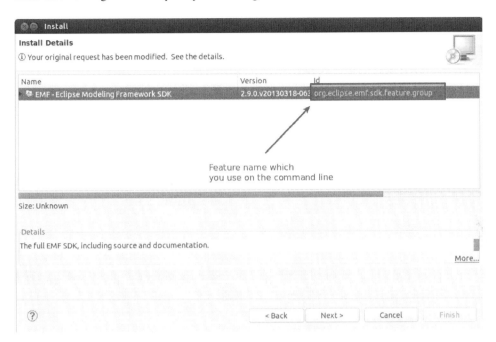

Part XI. Debugging with Eclipse

42

Introduction to debugging

42.1. What is debugging?

Debugging allows you to run a program interactively while watching the source code and the variables during the execution.

By *breakpoints* in the source code you specify where the execution of the program should stop. To stop the execution only if a field is read or modified, you can specify *watchpoints* .

Breakpoints and *watchpoints* can be summarized as *stop points*.

Once the program is stopped you can investigate variables, change their content, etc.

42.2. Debugging support in Eclipse

Eclipse allows you to start a Java program in *Debug mode*.

Eclipse has a special *Debug perspective* which gives you a preconfigured set of *views*. In this *perspective* you control the execution process of your program and can investigate the state of the variables.

43

Debugging in Eclipse

This chapter introduces the usage of the Eclipse Java debugger. You learn how to set breakpoints in your code and how to investigate the state of your program, e.g. by looking at current values of your variables.

43.1. Setting Breakpoints

To set breakpoints in your source code right-click in the small left margin in your source code editor and select *Toggle Breakpoint*. Alternatively you can double-click on this position.

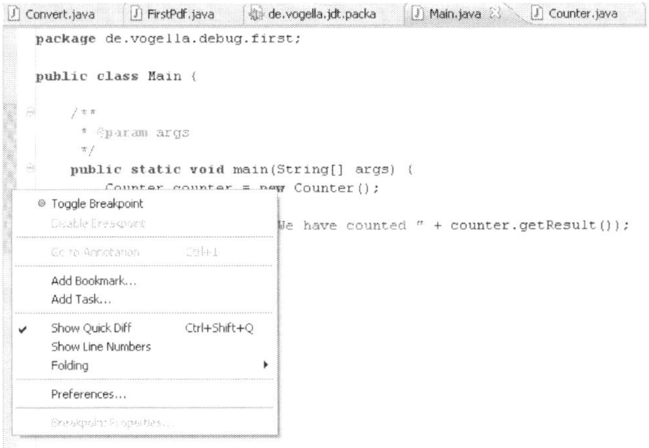

For example in the following screenshot we set a breakpoint on the line `Counter counter = new Counter();`.

```
Counter.java    Main.java ☒
  package de.vogella.debug.first;

  public class Main {

      /**
       * @param args
       */
      public static void main(String[] args) {
          Counter counter = new Counter();
          counter.count();
          System.out.println("We have counted " + counter.getResult());
      }

  }
```

43.2. Starting the Debugger

To debug your application, select a Java file which can be executed, right-click on it and select *Debug As → Java Application*.

After you have started the application once via the context menu, you can use the created launch configuration again via the *Debug* button in the Eclipse toolbar.

If you have not defined any breakpoints, this will run your program as normal. To debug the program you need to define breakpoints.

If you start the debugger, Eclipse asks you if you want to switch to the *Debug perspective* once a stop point is reached. Answer *Yes* in the corresponding dialog.

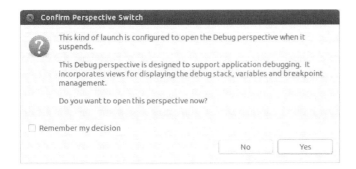

Afterwards Eclipse opens this *perspective*, which looks similar to the following screenshot.

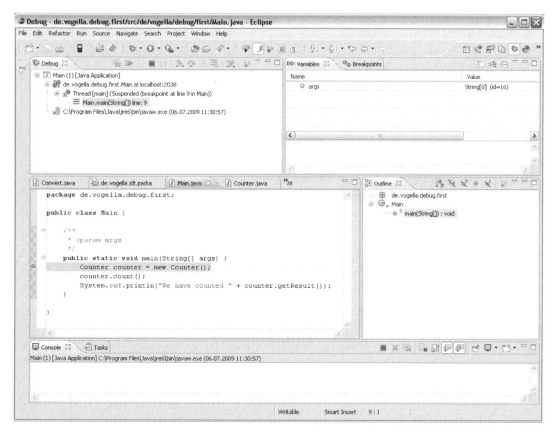

43.3. Controlling the program execution

Eclipse provides buttons in the toolbar for controlling the execution of the program you are debugging. Typically it is easier to use the corresponding keys to control this execution.

You can use the F5, F6, F7 and F8 key to step through your coding. The meaning of these keys is explained in the following table.

Table 43.1. Debugging key bindings / shortcuts

Key	Description
F5	Executes the currently selected line and goes to the next line in your program. If the selected line is a method call the debugger steps into the associated code.
F6	F6 steps over the call, i.e. it executes a method without stepping into it in the debugger.
F7	F7 steps out to the caller of the currently executed method. This finishes the execution of the current method and returns to the caller of this method.
F8	F8 tells the Eclipse debugger to resume the execution of the program code until is reaches the next breakpoint or watchpoint.

The following picture displays the buttons and their related keyboard shortcuts.

The call stack shows the parts of the program which are currently executed and how they relate to each other. The current stack is displayed in the *Debug view*.

43.4. Breakpoints view and deactivating breakpoints

The *Breakpoints view* allows you to delete and deactivate *stop points*, i.e. *breakpoints* and *watchpoints* and to modify their properties.

To deactivate a breakpoint, remove the corresponding checkbox in the *Breakpoints view*. To delete it you can use the corresponding buttons in the *view* toolbar. These options are depicted in the following screenshot.

If you want to deactivate all your breakpoints you can press the *Skip all breakpoints* button. If you press it again, your breakpoints are reactivated. This button is highlighted in the following screenshot.

43.5. Evaluating variables in the debugger

The *Variables view* displays fields and local variables from the current executing stack. Please note you need to run the debugger to see the variables in this *view*.

Use the drop-down menu to display static variables.

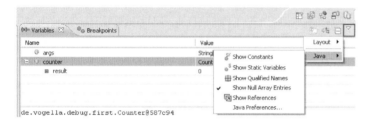

Via the drop-down menu of the *Variables view* you can customize the displayed columns. For example, you can show the actual type of each variable declaration. For this select *Layout → Select Columns...* → *Type*.

43.6. Changing variable assignments in the debugger

The *Variables view* allows you to change the values assigned to your variable at runtime. This is depicted in the following screenshot.

43.7. Controlling the display of the variables with Detail Formatter

By default the *Variables view* uses the `toString()` method to determine how to display the variable.

You can define a *Detail Formatter* in which you can use Java code to define how a variable is displayed.

For example the `toString()` method in the `Counter` class may show meaningless information, e.g. `de.vogella.combug.first.Counter@587c94`. To make this output more readable you can right-click on the corresponding variable and select the *New Detail Formater* entry from the context menu.

Afterwards you can use a method of this class to determine the output. In this example the `getResult()` method of this class is used. This setup is depicted in the following screenshot.

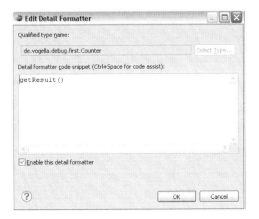

44

Advanced Debugging

The following chapter shows more options for debugging.

44.1. Breakpoint properties

After setting a breakpoint you can select the properties of the breakpoint, via *right-click → Breakpoint Properties*. Via the breakpoint properties you can define a condition that restricts the activation of this breakpoint.

You can for example specify that a breakpoint should only become active after it has reached 12 or more times via the *Hit Count* property.

You can also create a conditional expression. The execution of the program only stops at the breakpoint, if the condition evaluates to true. This mechanism can also be used for additional logging, as the code that specifies the condition is executed every time the program execution reaches that point.

The following screenshot depicts this setting.

44.2. Watchpoint

A *watchpoint* is a breakpoint set on a field. The debugger will stop whenever that field is read or changed.

You can set a *watchpoint* by double-clicking on the left margin, next to the field declaration. In the properties of a *watchpoint* you can configure if the execution should stop during read access (Field Access) or during write access (Field Modification) or both.

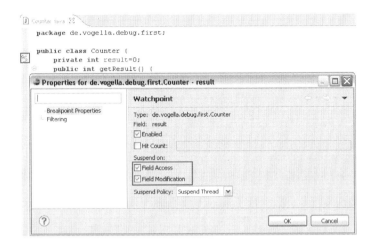

44.3. Exception breakpoints

You can set breakpoints which are triggered when exceptions in your Java source code are thrown. To define an exception breakpoint click on the *Add Java Exception Breakpoint* button icon in the *Breakpoints view* toolbar.

You can configure if the debugger should stop at caught or uncaught exceptions.

44.4. Method breakpoint

A method breakpoint is defined by double-clicking in the left margin of the editor next to the method header.

You can configure if you want to stop the program before entering or after leaving the method.

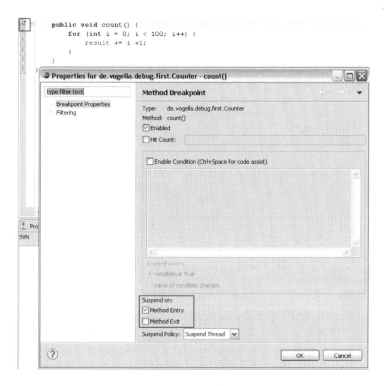

44.5. Breakpoints for loading classes

A class load breakpoint stops when the class is loaded.

To set a class load breakpoint, right-click on a class in the *Outline view* and choose the *Toggle Class Load Breakpoint* option.

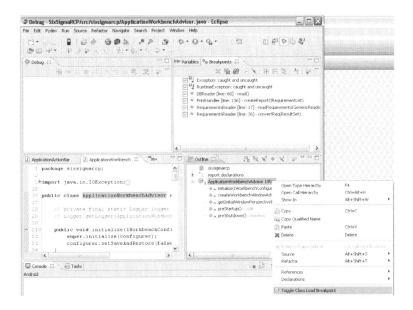

Alternative you can double-click in the left border of the Java editor beside the class definition.

44.6. Step Filter

You can define that certain packages should be skipped in debugging. This is for example useful if you use a framework for testing but don't want to step into the test framework classes. These packages can be configured via the *Window → Preferences → Java → Debug → Step Filtering* menu path.

44.7. Hit Count

For every breakpoint you can specify a hit count in its properties. The application is stopped once the breakpoint has been reached the number of times defined in the hit count.

44.8. Remote debugging

Eclipse allows you to debug applications which runs on another Java virtual machine or even on another machine.

To enable remote debugging you need to start your Java application with certain flags, as demonstrated in the following code example.

```
java -Xdebug -Xnoagent \
-Djava.compiler=NONE \
-Xrunjdwp:transport=dt_socket,server=y,suspend=y,address=5005
```

In you Eclipse IDE you can enter the hostname and port to connect for debugging via the *Run → Debug Configuration...* menu.

Here you can create a new debug configuration of the *Remote Java Application* type. This configuration allows you to enter the hostname and port for the connection as depicted in the following screenshot.

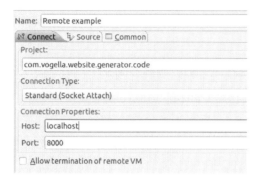

Note

Remote debugging requires that you have the source code of the application which is debugged available in your Eclipse IDE.

44.9. Drop to frame

Eclipse allows you to select any level (frame) in the call stack during debugging and set the JVM to restart from that point.

This allows you to rerun a part of your program. Be aware that variables which have been modified by code that already run will remain modified.

To use this feature, select a level in your stack and press the *Drop to Frame* button in the toolbar of the *Debug view*.

Note

Fields and external data may not be affected by the reset. For example if you write a entry to the database and afterward drop to a previous frame, this entry is still in the database.

The following screenshot depicts such a reset. If you restart your `for` loop, the field `result` is not set to its initial value and therefore the loop is not executed as without resetting the execution to a previous point.

```
package de.vogella.debug.first;

public class Counter {
    private int result = 0;

    public int getResult() {
        return result;
    }

    public void count() {
        for (int i = 0; i < 100; i++) {
            result += i + 1;
        }
    }
}
```

45

Exercise: Debugging

45.1. Create Project

To practice debugging create a new Java project called `de.vogella.combug.first`. Also create the package `de.vogella.combug.first` and create the following classes.

```java
package de.vogella.combug.first;

public class Counter {
  private int result = 0;

  public int getResult() {
    return result;
  }

  public void count() {
    for (int i = 0; i < 100; i++) {
      result += i + 1;
    }
  }
}
```

```java
package de.vogella.combug.first;

public class Main {
  /**
   * @param args
   */
  public static void main(String[] args) {
    Counter counter = new Counter();
    counter.count();
    System.out.println("We have counted "
        + counter.getResult());
  }
}
```

45.2. Debugging

Set a breakpoint in the `Counter` class. Debug your program and follow the execution of the `count` method.

Define a *Detailed Formatter* for your `Counter` which uses the `getResult` method. Debug your program again and verify that your new formatter is used.

Delete your breakpoint and add a breakpoint for class loading. Debug your program again and verify that the debugger stops when your class is loaded.

Part XII. Unit testing

46

Unit testing with JUnit

This chapter explains the concept of unit testing and how to use Eclipse for unit testing with the JUnit framework.

46.1. Unit tests and unit testing

A *unit test* is a piece of code written by a developer that executes a specific functionality in the code which is tested. The percentage of code which is tested by unit tests is typically called *test coverage*.

Unit tests target small units of code, e.g. a method or a class, (local tests) whereas *component and integration tests* targeting to test the behavior of a component or the integration between a set of components or a complete application consisting of several components.

Unit tests ensure that code works as intended. They are also very helpful to ensure that the code still works as intended in case you need to modify code for fixing a bug or extending functionality. Having a high test coverage of your code allows you to continue developing features without having to perform lots of manual tests.

Typically unit tests are created in their own project or their own source folder to avoid that the normal code and the test code is mixed.

46.2. Unit testing with JUnit

JUnit unit test in version 4.x is a test framework which uses annotations to identify methods that specify a test. Typically these test methods are contained in a class which is only used for testing. It is typically called a *Test class*.

The following code shows a JUnit test method which can be created via *File* → *New* → *JUnit* → *JUnit Test case*.

```
@Test
public void testMultiply() {

   // MyClass is tested
   MyClass tester = new MyClass();

   // Check if multiply(10,5) returns 50
   assertEquals("10 x 5 must be 50", 50, tester.multiply(10, 5));
}
```

JUnit assumes that all test methods can be executed in an arbitrary order. Therefore tests should not depend on other tests.

To write a test with JUnit you annotate a method with the `@org.junit.Test` annotation and use a method provided by JUnit to check the expected result of the code execution versus the actual result.

You can use the Eclipse user interface to run the test, via right-click on the test class and selecting *Run → Run As → JUnit Test*. Outside of Eclipse you can use `org.junit.runner.JUnitCore` class to run the test.

46.3. Available JUnit annotations

The following table gives an overview of the available annotations in JUnit 4.x.

Table 46.1. Annotations

Annotation	Description
@Test public void method()	The annotation @Test identifies that a method is a test method.
@Before public void method()	This method is executed before each test. This method can prepare the test environment (e.g. read input data, initialize the class).
@After public void method()	This method is executed after each test. This method can cleanup the test environment (e.g. delete temporary data, restore defaults). It can also save memory by cleaning up expensive memory structures.
@BeforeClass public static void method()	This method is executed once, before the start of all tests. This can be used to perform time intensive activities, for example to connect to a database. Methods annotated with this annotation need to be defined as `static` to work with JUnit.
@AfterClass public static void method()	This method is executed once, after all tests have been finished. This can be used to perform clean-up activities, for example to disconnect from a database. Methods annotated with this annotation need to be defined as `static` to work with JUnit.
@Ignore	Ignores the test method. This is useful when the underlying code has been changed and the test case has not yet been adapted. Or if the execution time of this test is too long to be included.
@Test (expected = Exception.class)	Fails, if the method does not throw the named exception.
@Test(timeout=100)	Fails, if the method takes longer than 100 milliseconds.

46.4. Assert statements

JUnit provides static methods in the `Assert` class to test for certain conditions. These methods typically start with `asserts` and allow you to specify the error message, the expected and the actual result. The following table gives an overview of these methods. Parameters in [] brackets are optional.

Table 46.2. Test methods

Statement	Description
fail(String)	Let the method fail. Might be used to check that a certain part of the code is not reached. Or to have a failing test before the test code is implemented.
assertTrue([message], boolean condition)	Checks that the boolean condition is true.
assertsEquals([String message], expected, actual)	Tests that two values are the same. Note: for arrays the reference is checked not the content of the arrays.
assertsEquals([String message], expected, actual, tolerance)	Test that float or double values match. The tolerance is the number of decimals which must be the same.
assertNull([message], object)	Checks that the object is null.
assertNotNull([message], object)	Checks that the object is not null.
assertSame([String], expected, actual)	Checks that both variables refer to the same object.
assertNotSame([String], expected, actual)	Checks that both variables refer to different objects.

Note

You should provide meaningful messages in assertions so that it is easier for the developer to identify the problem. This help in fixing the issue, especially if someone looks at the problem, which did not write the code under test or the test code.

46.5. Create a JUnit test suite

If you have several test classes you can combine them into a *test suite*. Running a test suite will execute all test classes in that suite.

The following example code shows a test suite which defines that two test classes should be executed. If you want to add another test class you can add it to @Suite.SuiteClasses statement.

```
package com.vogella.junit.first;

import org.junit.runner.RunWith;
import org.junit.runners.Suite;
import org.junit.runners.Suite.SuiteClasses;

@RunWith(Suite.class)
@SuiteClasses({ MyClassTest.class, MySecondClassTest.class })
public class AllTests {

}
```

46.6. Run your test outside Eclipse

Eclipse provides support for running your test interactively in the Eclipse IDE. You can also run your JUnit tests outside Eclipse via standard Java code. The `org.junit.runner.JUnitCore` class provides the `runClasses()` method which allows you to run one or several tests classes. As a return parameter you receive an object of the type `org.junit.runner.Result`. This object can be used to retrieve information about the tests.

In your `test` folder create a new class `MyTestRunner` with the following code. This class will execute your test class and write potential failures to the console.

```java
package de.vogella.junit.first;

import org.junit.runner.JUnitCore;
import org.junit.runner.Result;
import org.junit.runner.notification.Failure;

public class MyTestRunner {
  public static void main(String[] args) {
    Result result = JUnitCore.runClasses(MyClassTest.class);
    for (Failure failure : result.getFailures()) {
      System.out.println(failure.toString());
    }
  }
}
```

To run your JUnit tests outside Eclipse you need to add the JUnit library jar to the classpath of your program. Typically build frameworks like Apache Ant or Apache Maven are used to execute tests automatically on a regular basis.

47

Installation of JUnit

47.1. Using JUnit integrated into Eclipse

Eclipse allows you to use the version of JUnit which is integrated in Eclipse. If you use Eclipse no additional setup is required. In this case you can skip the following section.

47.2. Downloading the JUnit library

If you want to control the used JUnit library explicitly, download JUnit4.x.jar from the following JUnit website. The download contains the `junit-4.*.jar` which is the JUnit library. Add this library to your Java project and add it to the classpath.

```
http://junit.org/
```

48

Unit testing with Eclipse

48.1. Creating JUnit tests

You can write the JUnit tests manually but Eclipse supports the creation of JUnit tests via wizards.

For example to create a JUnit test or a test class for an existing class, right-click on your new class, select this class in the *Package Explorer view*, right-click on it and select *New → JUnit Test Case*.

Alternatively you can also use the JUnit wizards available under *File → New → Other... → Java → JUnit*.

48.2. Running JUnit tests

To run a test, select the class which contains the tests, right-click on it and select *Run-as → JUnit Test*. This starts JUnit and executes all test methods in this class.

Eclipse provides the **Alt+Shift+X, ,T** shortcut to run the test in the selected class. If you position the cursor on one method name, this shortcut runs only the selected test method.

To see the result of an JUnit test, Eclipse uses the *JUnit view* which shows the results of the tests. You can also select individual unit test in this *view*, right-click them and select *Run* to execute them again.

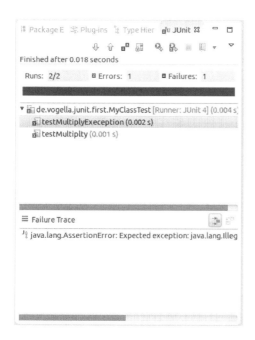

By default this *view* shows all tests you can also configure, that it shows only failing tests.

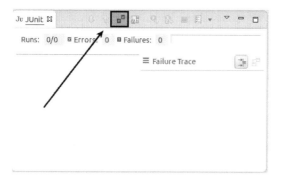

You can also define that the *view* is only activated if you have a failing test.

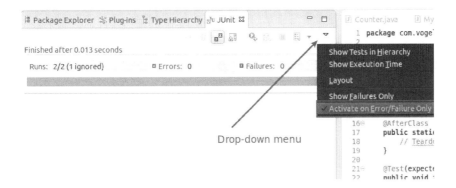

Drop-down menu

Note

Eclipse creates run configurations for tests. You can see and modify these via the *Run →
Run Configurations...* menu.

48.3. JUnit static imports

JUnit uses static methods and Eclipse cannot always create the corresponding `static import`
statements automatically.

You can make the JUnit test methods available via the *Content Assists*. *Content Assists* is a functionality
in Eclipse which allows the developer to get context sensitive code completion in an editor upon user
request.

Open the Preferences via *Window → Preferences* and select *Java → Editor → Content Assist →
Favorites*.

Use the new *New Type* button to add the `org.junit.Assert` type. This makes for example
the `assertTrue`, `assertFalse` and `assertEquals` methods directly available in the *Content
Assists*.

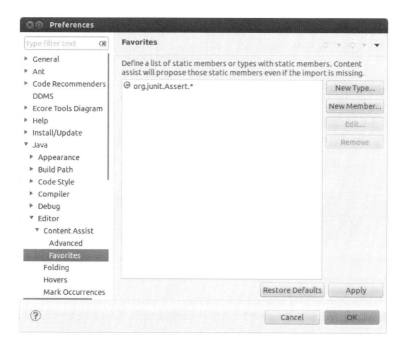

You can now use *Content Assists* (shortcut: **Ctrl+Space**) to add the method and the import.

48.4. Wizard for creating test suites

To create a test suite in Eclipse you select the test classes which should be included into this in the *Package Explorer view*, right-click on them and select *New* → *Other...* → *JUnit* → *JUnit Test Suite*.

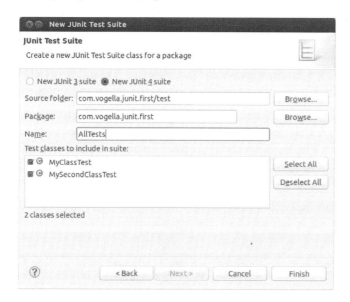

48.5. Testing exception

The @Test (expected = Exception.class) annotation is limited as it can only test for one exception. To test exceptions you can use the following test pattern.

```
try {
    mustThrowException();
    fail();
} catch (Exception e) {
    // expected
    // could also check for message of exception, etc.
}
```

Exercise: Using JUnit

49.1. Project preparation

Create a new project called *com.vogella.junit.first*.

Create a new source folder test. For this right-click on your project, select *Properties* and choose the *Java Build Path* . Select the *Source* tab.

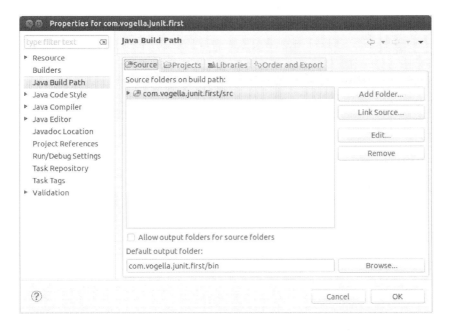

Press the *Add Folder* button, afterwards press the *Create New Folder* button. Create the test folder.

The result is depicted in the following sceenshot.

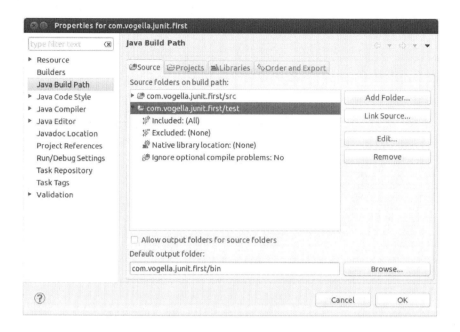

Alternatively you can add a new source folder by right-clicking on a project and selecting *New* →
Source Folder.

49.2. Create a Java class

In the `src` folder, create the `com.vogella.junit.first` package and the following class.

```java
package com.vogella.junit.first;

public class MyClass {
  public int multiply(int x, int y) {
    // the following is just an example
    if (x > 999) {
      throw new IllegalArgumentException("X should be less than 1000");
    }
    return x / y;
  }
}
```

49.3. Create a JUnit test

Right-click on your new class in the *Package Explorer view* and select *New → JUnit Test Case*.

In the following wizard ensure that the *New JUnit 4 test* flag is selected and set the source folder to
`test`, so that your test class gets created in this folder.

Press the *Next* button and select the methods that you want to test.

If the JUnit library is not part of the classpath of your project, Eclipse will prompt you to add it. Use this to add JUnit to your project.

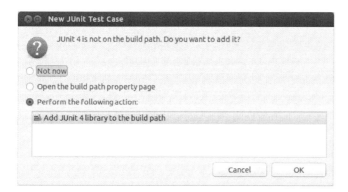

Create a test with the following code.

```
package com.vogella.junit.first;

import static org.junit.Assert.assertEquals;

import org.junit.AfterClass;
```

```
import org.junit.BeforeClass;
import org.junit.Test;

public class MyClassTest {

  @BeforeClass
  public static void testSetup() {
  }

  @AfterClass
  public static void testCleanup() {
    // Teardown for data used by the unit tests
  }

  @Test(expected = IllegalArgumentException.class)
  public void testExceptionIsThrown() {
    MyClass tester = new MyClass();
    tester.multiply(1000, 5);
  }

  @Test
  public void testMultiply() {
    MyClass tester = new MyClass();
    assertEquals("10 x 5 must be 50", 50, tester.multiply(10, 5));
  }
}
```

49.4. Run your test in Eclipse

Right-click on your new test class and select *Run-As* → *JUnit Test*.

The result of the tests will be displayed in the JUnit *view*. In our example one test should be succesful and one test should show an error. This error is indicated by a red bar.

The test is failing because our multiplier class is currently not working correctly. It does a division instead of multiplication. Fix the bug and re-run test to get a green bar.

50

Advanced JUnit options

50.1. Parameterized test

JUnit allows you to use parameters in a tests class. This class can contain one test method and this method is executed with the different parameters provided.

You mark a test class as a parameterized test with the @RunWith(Parameterized.class) annotation.

Such a test class must contain a static method annotated with @Parameters that generates and returns a Collection of Arrays. Each item in this collection is used as the parameters for the test method.

You need also to create a constructor in which you store the values for each test. The number of elements in each array provided by the method annotated with @Parameters must correspond to the number of parameters in the constructor of the class. The class is created for each parameter and the test values are passed via the constructor to the class.

The following code shows an example for a parameterized test. It assume that you test the multiply() method of the MyClass class which was used in an example earlier.

```java
package de.vogella.junit.first;

import static org.junit.Assert.assertEquals;

import java.util.Arrays;
import java.util.Collection;

import org.junit.Test;
import org.junit.runner.RunWith;
import org.junit.runners.Parameterized;
import org.junit.runners.Parameterized.Parameters;

@RunWith(Parameterized.class)
public class MyParameterizedClassTest {

  private int multiplier;

  public MyParameterizedClassTest(int testParameter) {
    this.multiplier = testParameter;
  }

  // Creates the test data
```

```
@Parameters
public static Collection<Object[]> data() {
   Object[][] data = new Object[][] { { 1 }, { 5 }, { 121 } };
   return Arrays.asList(data);
}

@Test
public void testMultiplyException() {
   MyClass tester = new MyClass();
   assertEquals("Result", multiplier * multiplier,
        tester.multiply(multiplier, multiplier));
}

}
```

If you run this test class, the test method is executed with each defined parameter. In the above example the test method is executed three times.

50.2. Rules

Via the @Rule annotation you can create objects which can be used and configured in your test methods. This adds more flexibility to your tests. You could for example specify which exception message your expect during execution of your test code.

```
package de.vogella.junit.first;

import org.junit.Rule;
import org.junit.Test;
import org.junit.rules.ExpectedException;

public class RuleExceptionTesterExample {

   @Rule
   public ExpectedException exception = ExpectedException.none();

   @Test
   public void throwsIllegalArgumentExceptionIfIconIsNull() {
      exception.expect(IllegalArgumentException.class);
      exception.expectMessage("Negative value not allowed");
      ClassToBeTested t = new ClassToBeTested();
      t.methodToBeTest(-1);
   }
}
```

JUnit provides already several useful implementations of rules. For example the TemporaryFolder class allows to setup files and folders which are automatically removed after a test.

The following code shows an example for the usage of the TemporaryFolder implementation.

```
package de.vogella.junit.first;

import static org.junit.Assert.assertTrue;

import java.io.File;
```

```java
import java.io.IOException;

import org.junit.Rule;
import org.junit.Test;
import org.junit.rules.TemporaryFolder;

public class RuleTester {

    @Rule
    public TemporaryFolder folder = new TemporaryFolder();

    @Test
    public void testUsingTempFolder() throws IOException {
        File createdFolder = folder.newFolder("newfolder");
        File createdFile = folder.newFile("myfilefile.txt");
        assertTrue(createdFile.exists());
    }
}
```

To write your own rule you need to implement the `TestRule` interface.

51

Testing with mock objects

51.1. Testing with mock objects

The process of *Unit testing* is defined as testing classes or methods in isolation.

Java classes usually depend on other classes. A *mock object* is a dummy implementation for an interface or a class in which you define the output of certain method calls. Mock objects allow you to unit test the class which should be tested without any dependencies.

You can create these mock objects manually (via code) or use a mock framework to simulate these classes. Mock frameworks allow you to create mock objects at runtime and define their behavior.

The classical example for a mock object is a a data provider. In production a real database is used but for testing a mock object simulates the database and ensures that the test conditions are always the same.

These mock objects can be provided to the class which is tested. Therefore the class to be tested should avoid any hard dependency on external data.

Mock frameworks also allow to test the expected interaction with the mock object, e.g. you test which methods have been called on the mock object.

51.2. Mock frameworks

Popular mock frameworks are EasyMock, jMock and Mockito. The following lists the links to these frameworks.

```
#jMock
http://jmock.org/

# EasyMock
http://easymock.org/

# Mockito
http://code.google.com/p/mockito/
```

52

EasyMock

52.1. EasyMock

EasyMock is a mock framework which can be easily used in conjunction with JUnit. The following description demonstrates the usage of EasyMock.

EasyMock instantiates an object based on an interface or class.

```
// ICalcMethod is the object which is mocked
ICalcMethod calcMethod = EasyMock.createMock(ICalcMethod.class);
```

EasyMock has several methods which are used to configure the Mock object. The `expect()` method tells EasyMock to simulate a method with certain arguments. The `andReturn()` method defines the return value of this method for the specified method parameters. The `times()` method defines how often the Mock object will be called.

The `replay()` method is called to make the Mock object available.

```
// setup the mock object
expect(calcMethod.calc(Position.BOSS)).andReturn(70000.0).times(2);
expect(calcMethod.calc(Position.PROGRAMMER)).andReturn(50000.0);
// Setup is finished need to activate the mock
replay(calcMethod);
```

52.2. Download Easy Mock

Download EasyMock from the EasyMock Homepage and add the `easymock.jar` library to your classpath.

```
http://easymock.org/
```

You also need to download the Objenesis [http://objenesis.googlecode.com/svn/docs/download.html] and Cglib [http://cglib.sourceforge.net/] libraries and add these `jars` to your classpath.

53

Tutorial: Using Easy Mock and JUnit

53.1. Create project and classes

Create a new Java Project called *com.vogella.testing.easymock.first*. Create the following classes.

```java
package com.vogella.testing.easymock.first;

public enum Position {
    BOSS, PROGRAMMER, SURFER
}
```

```java
package com.vogella.testing.easymock.first;

public interface ICalcMethod {
    double calc(Position position);
}
```

```java
package com.vogella.testing.easymock.first;

public class IncomeCalculator {

    private ICalcMethod calcMethod;
    private Position position;

    public void setCalcMethod(ICalcMethod calcMethod) {
        this.calcMethod = calcMethod;
    }

    public void setPosition(Position position) {
        this.position = position;
    }

    public double calc() {
        if (calcMethod == null) {
            throw new RuntimeException("CalcMethod not yet maintained");
        }
        if (position == null) {
            throw new RuntimeException("Position not yet maintained");
        }
        return calcMethod.calc(position);
    }
}
```

The `IncomeCalculator` class should be tested. The class has the purpose to calculate the salary of a person based on the provided method and position. Obviously the test depends on the provided methods.

53.2. Create tests

Create a new `test` source folder in your project.

Create a new test for `IncomeCalculator` and place the new test class in this folder.

```java
package com.vogella.testing.easymock.first.test;
// Use static imports to
// have direct access to these methods
import static org.easymock.EasyMock.expect;
import static org.easymock.EasyMock.replay;
import static org.easymock.EasyMock.verify;
import static org.junit.Assert.assertEquals;
import static org.junit.Assert.fail;

import org.easymock.EasyMock;
import org.junit.Before;
import org.junit.Test;

import com.vogella.testing.easymock.first.ICalcMethod;
import com.vogella.testing.easymock.first.IncomeCalculator;
import com.vogella.testing.easymock.first.Position;

public class IncomeCalculatorTest {

    private ICalcMethod calcMethod;
    private IncomeCalculator calc;

    @Before
    public void setUp() throws Exception {
        calcMethod = EasyMock.createMock(ICalcMethod.class);
        calc = new IncomeCalculator();
    }

    @Test
    public void testCalc1() {
        // Setting up the expected value of the method call calc
        expect(calcMethod.calc(Position.BOSS)).andReturn(70000.0).times(2);
        expect(calcMethod.calc(Position.PROGRAMMER)).andReturn(50000.0);
        // Setup is finished need to activate the mock
        replay(calcMethod);

        calc.setCalcMethod(calcMethod);
        try {
            calc.calc();
            fail("Exception did not occur");
        } catch (RuntimeException e) {

        }
        calc.setPosition(Position.BOSS);
        assertEquals(70000.0, calc.calc(), 0);
        assertEquals(70000.0, calc.calc(), 0);
        calc.setPosition(Position.PROGRAMMER);
        assertEquals(50000.0, calc.calc(), 0);
```

```java
        calc.setPosition(Position.SURFER);
        verify(calcMethod);
    }

    @Test(expected = RuntimeException.class)
    public void testNoCalc() {
        calc.setPosition(Position.SURFER);
        calc.calc();
    }

    @Test(expected = RuntimeException.class)
    public void testNoPosition() {
        expect(calcMethod.calc(Position.BOSS)).andReturn(70000.0);
        replay(calcMethod);
        calc.setCalcMethod(calcMethod);
        calc.calc();
    }

    @Test(expected = RuntimeException.class)
    public void testCalc2() {
        // Setting up the expected value of the method call calc
        expect(calcMethod.calc(Position.SURFER)).
            andThrow(new RuntimeException("Don't know this guy")).times(1);

        // Setup is finished need to activate the mock
        replay(calcMethod);
        calc.setPosition(Position.SURFER);
        calc.setCalcMethod(calcMethod);
        calc.calc();
    }

}
```

After execution of the test you can call the `verify` method to check if the mock object was called as defined.

Part XIII. Task Management with Mylyn

54

What is Mylyn?

This chapter introduces the *Eclipse Mylyn* software component for local task management.

54.1. Motivation of Mylyn

Software developers perform a variety of activities. They write source code for new functionality, fix bugs, write documentation, answer questions, attend meetings and much more.

Developing software in the Eclipse IDE involves writing new classes or methods and modifying existing code.

For example the procedure of fixing a bug may involve writing unit tests, refactoring existing code, reading and searching involved code and finally fixing the affected code. If the activity of the developer during this task is interrupted or if the developer has to work on another task, e.g. an urgent bug, he loses the *context* he built while working on the previous task , i.e. all the involved classes which he has opened in the Eclipse IDE.

Eclipse Mylyn is a software component packaged with the Eclipse IDE. The idea of Mylyn is to preserve the current state of the Eclipse IDE, e.g. the *context*, in a *task*.

Eclipse Mylyn allows the developer to record his activities in such a task while he is working on it. Each task has a *context* which captures the involved classes, methods and the cursor position in the opened Java or text *editor*.

When switching between tasks, the corresponding context is restored and the editors which belong to this tasks are opened and the others are closed.

Mylyn can also filter information in the IDE. For example, the *Package Explorer view* can be set to show only the files relevant for the current task.

This functionality sounds simple but helps finding the right information much faster during a task switch of the developer.

54.2. Task tracker integration

It is also possible to integrate Mylyn with bug tracking solutions. For example you can integrate Mylyn with the *Bugzilla* bugtracker system or with the issue system of the *Github* website.

In this case, tasks and the content of these tasks can be shared among developers. This is even more powerful but will not be described here, as there are lots of different bug tracking systems and the integration to them is rapidly changing.

54.3. Scope of this description

This book describes the usage of Mylyn for managing local tasks and describes the usage of the *Bugzilla* bugtracker integration for Eclipse.org.

There are a huge variety of available issue trackers it is beyond the scope of this book to cover all of them. Information about the integration with the different trackers can be found on the Mylyn homepage.

```
http://www.eclipse.org/mylyn/
```

54.4. Installation

Most Eclipse downloads contain Mylyn already. If you need to install it you can use the *update manager* via *Help → Install new Software...* and install Mylyn from the update site or your release. The following screenshot shows this for the Kepler release.

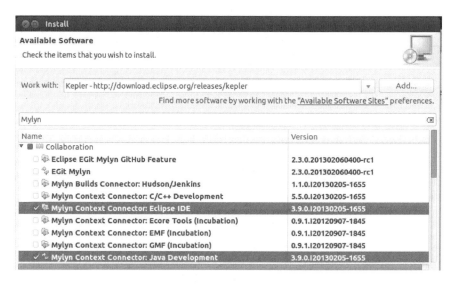

55

Using Mylyn

55.1. Task List view

The *Task List view* is part of the standard Java *perspective*.

In case you closed the *view*, you can re-open it via *Window → Show View → Mylyn → Task List*.

55.2. Create new tasks

To create a new task press the *New Task* button or right-click in the *Task List view* and select *New → Task*.

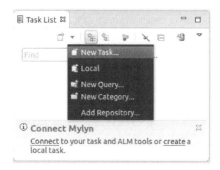

Select the *Local* repository, as depicted in the following screenshot.

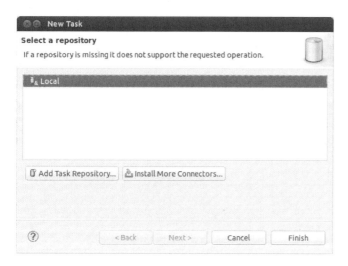

55.3. Activate a task

To start working on a task, select the *Activate task* button. If the task has already captured a *context*, Mylyn filters the visible elements in the *Package Explorer view*.

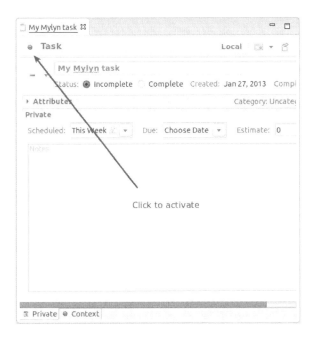

You can remove the filter in the *Package Explorer view* by clicking the *Focus on Active Task* button in the toolbar of this *view*. Afterwards all files are displayed.

If you open a file while having an activated task, this file is added to the context of the task.

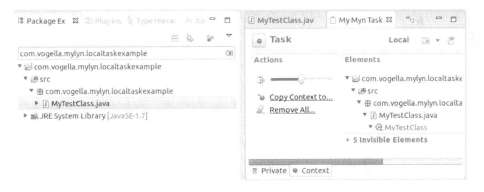

Once you have identified all necessary elements, you can focus again on the task to filter out the unnecessary elements.

If you have to switch to another task you simply can activate it. The context of the task will be restored.

55.4. Create task from Problems view

You can create a new Mylyn task from the *Problems view*, by right-clicking on a problem and selecting *New Task from Marker...* from the context menu.

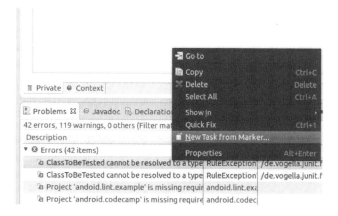

55.5. Export and import your tasks

Mylyn allows you to export and import your local tasks. Select your categories or tasks in the *Task List view*, right-click on them and select *Export and Import* from the context menu.

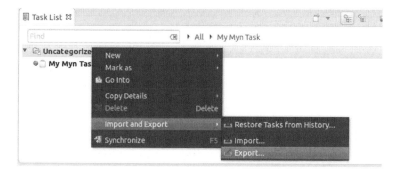

56

Bugzilla integration

56.1. Mylyn and tracker integration

Mylyn allows to connect to bug tracking software and in most cases to share the task context with others via the bugtracker. Mylyn supports many bugtrackers, e.g. Github, Jira or Bugzilla.

The following description explains how you can use Mylyn to work on bugs and feature requests which are tracked in the Eclipse *Bugzilla* installation.

56.2. Eclipse Bugzilla

All known Eclipse bugs and feature requests are stored in the Eclipse Bugzilla database which can be found under the following link.

```
https://bugs.eclipse.org/bugs/
```

Mylyn has build in support for the Eclipse bug database. Just right click in the *Task List view* and select *New → Query*.

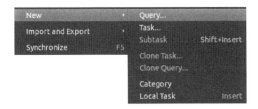

Select the *Eclipse* entry and press the *Next* button.

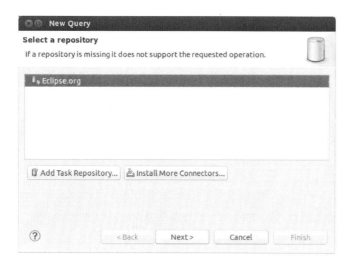

Select the *Create query* entry and *Create query using form*.

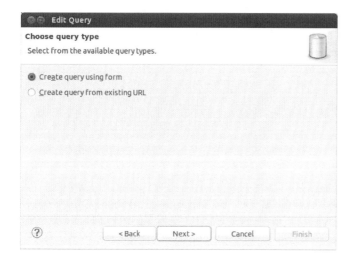

If for example you want to see all open bugs in Platform - UI then you could enter a query as depicted in the following screenshot.

If you now activate a task, you can use Mylyn to work on Eclipse bugs.

Part XIV. Using Git with Eclipse

57

Introduction to Git

The following chapter gives an overview of what Git is about and how it works.

57.1. What is a version control system?

A version control system allows you to track the history of a collection of files and includes the functionality to revert the collection of files to another version. Each version captures a snapshot of the file system at a certain point in time. The collection of files is usually *source code* for a programming language but a typical version control system can put any type of file under version control.

The collection of files and their complete history are stored in a *repository*.

The process of creating different versions (snapshots) in the repository is depicted in the following graphic. Please note that this picture fits primarily to Git, another version control systems like CVS don't create snapshots but store deltas.

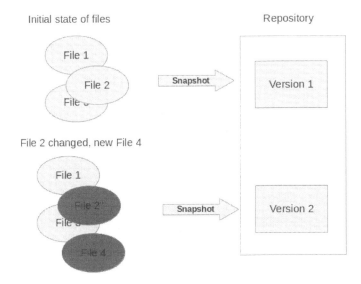

These snapshots can be used to change your collection of files. You may, for example, revert the collection of files to a state from 2 days ago. Or you may switch between versions for experimental features.

57.2. What is a distributed version control system?

A distributed version control system has not necessary a central server which stores the data.

The user can copy an existing *repository*. This copying process is typically called *cloning* in a distributed version control system.

Typically there is a central server for keeping a repository but each cloned repository is a full copy of this repository. The decision which of the copies is considered to be the central server repository is a pure convention and not tied to the capabilities of the distributed version control itself.

Every local copy contains the full history of the collection of files and a cloned repository has the same functionality as the original repository.

Every repository can exchange versions of the files with other repositories by transporting these changes. This is typically done via the selected central server repository.

57.3. What is Git?

Git is a distributed version control system.

Git originates from the Linux kernel development and is used by many popular Open Source projects, e.g. the Android or the Eclipse Open Source projects, as well as by many commercial organizations.

The core of Git was originally written in the programming language *C* but Git has also been re-implemented in other languages, e.g. Java and Python.

57.4. Local repository and operations

After cloning or creating a repository the user has a complete copy of the repository. The user performs version control operations against this local repository, e.g. create new versions, revert changes, etc.

There are two types of Git repositories:

• bare repositories used on servers to share changes coming from different developers

• working repositories which allow you to create new changes through modification of files and to create new versions in the repository

If you want to delete a Git repository, you can simply delete the folder which contains the repository.

57.5. Remote repositories

Git allows the user to synchronize the local repository with other (remote) repositories.

Users with sufficient authorization can *push* changes from their local repository to remote repositories. They can also *fetch* or *pull* changes from other repositories to their local Git repository.

57.6. Branching and merging

Git supports *branching* which means that you can work on different versions of your collection of files in parallel. For example if you want to develop a new feature, you can create a branch and make the changes in this branch without affecting the state of your files in another branch.

Branches in Git are local. A branch created in a local repository, which was cloned from another repository, does not need to have a counterpart in the remote repository. Local branches can be compared with *remote tracking branches* which proxy the state of branches in another remote repository.

Git supports that changes from different branches can be combined. This allows the developer for example to work independently on a branch called *production* for bugfixes and another branch called *feature_123* for implementing a new feature. The developer can use Git commands to combine the changes at a later point in time.

For example the Linux kernel community used to share code corrections (patches) via mailing lists to combine changes coming from different developers. Git is a system which allows developers to automate such a process.

57.7. Working tree

The user works on a collection of files which may originate from a certain point in time of the repository. The user may also create new files or change and delete existing ones. The current collection of files is called the *working tree*.

A standard Git repository contains the *working tree* (single checkout of one version of the project) and the full history of the repository. You can work in this *working tree* by modifying content and committing the changes to the Git repository.

57.8. How to add changes to your Git repository

If you modify your *working tree*, e.g. by adding a new file or by changing an existing file, you need to perform two steps in Git to persist the changes in the Git repository.

First you need to mark them to be relevant for Git. Marking changes as relevant for the version control is called *staging* or *to add them to the staging area*.

Note

The *staging area* term is currently preferred by the Git community over the old *index* term. Both terms mean the same thing.

By adding a file to the *staging area* you store a snapshot of this file in the Git repository. After adding the selected files to the *staging area*, you store this change in the Git repository.

Storing the changes in the Git repository is called *committing*. You commit the staged changes to create a new snapshot (commit) of the complete working tree in the Git repository.

For example, if you change a file you can store a snapshot of this file in the *staging area* with the `git add` command. This allows you to incrementally modify files, stage them, modify and stage them again until you are satisfied with your changes. Afterwards you commit the staged changes in order to capture a new snapshot of the complete relevant files. For this you use the `git commit` command.

This process is depicted in the following graphic.

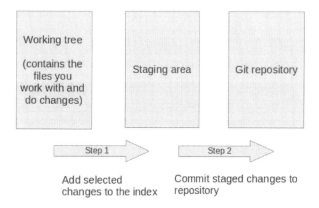

57.9. Committing and commit objects

If you commit changes to your Git repository, you create a new *commit object* in the Git repository. This commit object is addressable via a *SHA-1 checksum*. This checksum is 40 character long and is a secure hash of the content of the files, the content of the directories, the complete history of up to the new commit, the committer and several other factors.

This means that Git is safe, you cannot manipulate a file in the Git repository without Git noticing that *SHA-1 checksum* does not fit anymore to the content.

The *commit object* points via a *tree* object to the individual files in this commit. The files are stored in the Git repository as *blob* objects and might be compressed by Git for better performance.

Such a commit object is depicted in the following picture.

Commit ID (SHA-1 Hash)
Tree object: ID ─────────►
Author: Lars Vogel
Committer: Lars Vogel
Commit Message: Initial commit

Snapshot of the file system

58

Writing good commit messages

58.1. Importance of Git commit messages

A *commit* adds a new version to the repository. This version is described by a *commit message*.

The *commit message* describes the changes recorded in a commit and helps the user to understand the history of a files contained in a Git repository.

A commit message should therefore be descriptive and informative without repeating the code changes.

58.2. Guidelines for useful commit messages

A commit message should have a header and a body. The header should be less than 50 characters and the body should wrap its text at 72 so that the commit message is displayed well on the command line or in graphical tools displaying the history. The body should be separated from the header by an empty line.

The body should mainly describe the reason why the change was made. The changes in the file can be reviewed with the help of Git.

The commit message should be in present tense, e.g. "Add better error handling" instead of "Added better error handling".

The last parameter can also contain *metadata* as key-value pairs. This metadata can be used to trigger certain behavior. For example the *Gerrit* code review system uses the `Change-Id` key followed by the commit id to identify to which review the message belongs.

58.3. Example message

The following can serve as an example for a commit message.

```
Short summary (less than 50 characters)

Detailed explanation, if required, line break at around 72 characters
more stuff to describe...

Fixes: bug #8009
Change-Id: 26b5f96ccb7b2293dc9b7a5cba0760294afba9fd
```

58.4. Example histories

The following listing shows the history of a Git repository with bad commit messages. This history is not useful.

```
21a8456 update
29f4219 update
016c696 update
29bc541 update
740a130 initial commit
```

The next listing shows the history of another Git repository in which better commit messages have been used. This history give already a good overview about the activities.

```
7455823 bug 391086: Search and filter the model editor tree.
9a84a8a [404207] Missing DynamicMenuContribution in child selector
952e014 [404187] Spelling error in Toolbar/Add child
71eeea9 bug 402875: Importing model elements from legacy RCP
123672c Bug 403679 - New Application wizard is missing dependencies
97cdb9a Bug 388635 creates an id for handlers
```

59

Tools and terminology overview

59.1. Tools

The tooling for Git is originally based on the command line. These days there is a huge variety of available Git tools.

You can use graphical tools, for example *EGit* for the Eclipse IDE.

59.2. Terminology

The following table provides a summary of important *Git* terminology.

Table 59.1. Git Terminology

Term	Definition
Repository	A *repository* contains the history, the different versions over time and all different branches and tags. In Git each copy of the repository is a complete repository. If the repository is not a bare repository, it allows you to checkout revisions into your working tree.
Working tree	The *working tree* contains the content of a commit which you can checkout from the Git repository. You can modify the content and commit the changes again to the Git repository.
Branches	A *branch* is a named pointer to a commit. Selecting a branch in Git terminology is called *to checkout a branch*. If you are working in a certain branch, the creation of a new commit advances this pointer to the newly created commit. Each commit knows its successor or successors. This way a branch defines its own line of descents in the overall version graph formed by all commits in the repository. You can create a new branch from an existing one and change the code independently from other branches. One of the branches is the default (typically named *master*).
Tags	A tag points to a commit which uniquely identifies a version of the Git repository. With a tag, you can have a named point to which you can always revert, e.g. the coding of 25.01.2009 in the branch "testing". Branches and tags are named pointers, the difference is that branches move when a new commit is created while tags always point to the same commit.

Term	Definition
Commit	You commit your changes into a repository. This creates a new *commit object* in the Git repository which uniquely identifies a new revision of the content of the repository. This revision can be retrieved later, for example if you want to see the source code of an older version. Each commit object contains the author and the committer, thus making it possible to identify the source of the change. The author and committer might be different people.
URL	A URL in Git determines the location of the repository.
Revision	Represents a version of the source code. Git implements revisions as *commit objects* (or short *commits*). These are identified by a SHA-1 secure hash. SHA-1 ids are 160 bits long and are represented in hexadecimal.
HEAD	*HEAD* is a symbolic link most often pointing to the currently checked out branch. Sometimes, e.g. when directly checking out a commit *HEAD* points to a commit, this is called *detached HEAD mode*. In that state creation of a commit will not move any branch. The versions before that can be addressed via *HEAD~1*, *HEAD~2* and so on. If you switch branches the *HEAD* pointer moves to the last commit in the branch. If you checkout a specific commit the *HEAD* points to this commit.
Staging area	The *staging area* is the place to store changes in the working tree before the commit. It contains the set of changes relevant for the next commit.
Index	*Index* is an alternative term for the *staging area*

60

Using Git in Eclipse

This chapter introduces EGit which provides integrated tooling for working with Git repositories within Eclipse.

60.1. Scope of this descriptioin

Note

This description contains sufficient information about working with Git in Eclipse but it does not cover all concepts for Git.

For a detailed description of the Git concepts and different options please see the following link or the corresponding Git book from Lars Vogel: Mastering the Git command line from Lars Vogel [http://www.vogella.com/articles/Git/article.html]

60.2. What is EGit

EGit is an Eclipse plug-in (software component) which allows you to use the distributed version control system *Git* directly within the Eclipse IDE.

EGit is based on the *JGit* library. *JGit* is a library which implements the *Git* functionality in Java.

60.3. Installation of Git into Eclipse

The *EGit* plug-in can be installed into every Eclipse IDE installation. Usually EGit supports the last two Eclipse releases.

Most Eclipse 4.2 and Eclipse 4.3 downloads from Eclipse.org contain *EGit* in their default configuration. In this case no additional installation is required.

If the *EGit* plug-in is missing in your Eclipse installation, you can install it via the Eclipse installation manager. Start this manager via the *Help → Install new Software* menu entry.

EGit can be installed from the following URL:

```
http://download.eclipse.org/egit/updates
```

The dialog to install EGit is depicted in the following screenshot.

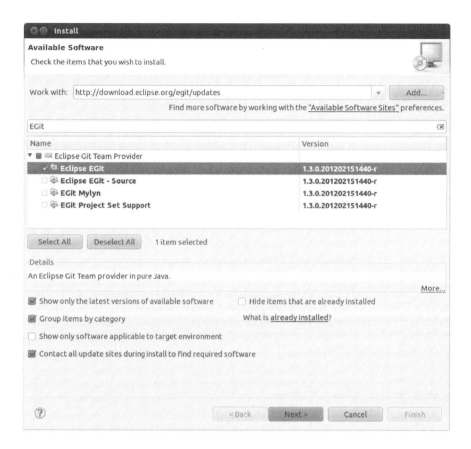

60.4. Setting up Git in Eclipse

60.4.1. Eclipse preferences

Before using EGit you should configure your name and email address which is used to fill the author and committer information of commits you create.

Git configuration settings can be configured using the EGit configuration preference page but this configuration is not stored in the Eclipse preference store but in git configuration files in order to ensure that native git sees the same configuration.

The Eclipse Git functionality allows you to configure your default user and email address for a commit. Select *Window → Preferences → Team → Git → Configuration* to set them up.

You can add entries to your Git configuration by pressing the *Add Entries* button on the *Git Configuration* preference page. To add your user, use the `user.name` as key and your real name as value. Repeat the procedure for your email address.

You can add more values in this dialog. These values are stored in the same way the Git command line would store them, so that you can use EGit and Git for the same Git repository.

You can also enter the default folder for storing Git repositories via the *Window → Preferences → Git → Team → Default Repository Folder* entry.

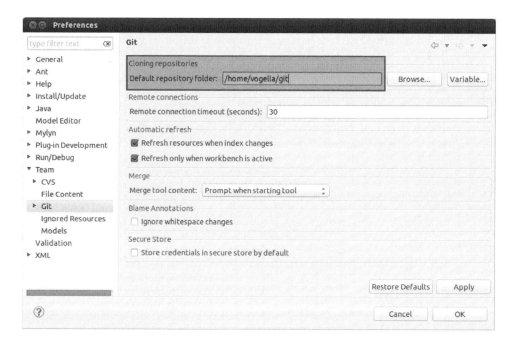

Note

You can also use Eclipse configuration variables to define this path, e.g. if you want to store repositories in the folder "git" under the Eclipse workspace you may use ${workspace_loc}/git.

Eclipse also supports the `.gitignore` file for excluding certain files from the Git repository.

60.4.2. Ignore certain files

Git can be configured to ignore certain files and directories. This is configured by placing the `.gitignore` file. This file can be in any directory and can contain patterns for files. For example, you can tell Git to ignore the `bin` directory via the following `.gitignore` file in the root directory of the working tree.

You can use certain wildcards in this file. `*` matches several characters. The `?` parameter matches one character.

```
# Ignore all bin directories
bin
# Ignore all files ending with ~
*~
# Ignore the target directory
# Matches "target" in any subfolder
target/
```

You can also setup a global .gitignore file valid for all Git repositories via the core.excludesfile setting. The setup of this setting is demonstrated in the following code snippet.

```
# Create a ~/.gitignore in your user directory
cd ~/
touch .gitignore

# Exclude bin and .metadata directories
echo "bin" >> .gitignore
echo ".metadata" >> .gitignore
echo "*~" >> .gitignore
echo "target/" >> .gitignore

# Configure Git to use this file
# as global .gitignore

git config --global core.excludesfile ~/.gitignore
```

The local .gitignore file can be committed into the Git repository and therefore is visible to everyone who clones the repository. The global .gitignore file is only locally visible.

Note

Files that are committed to the Git repository are not automatically removed if you add them to a .gitignore file.

60.4.3. Activating the Git toolbar

To simplify access to the common Git operations you can activate the Git toolbar. For this select *Window* → *Customize perspective...* and check the command groups *Git* and *Git Navigation Actions* in the *Command Groups Availability* tab.

61

Working with a local Git repository in Eclipse

61.1. Introduction

The following section explains how to create a local Git repository for one project with Eclipse. This allows you to keep track of your changes in the project and allows you to revert to another state at a later point in time.

61.2. Creating an Eclipse project

Create a new Java project called *de.vogella.git.first* in Eclipse. Create the `de.vogella.git.first` package and the following class.

```
package de.vogella.git.first;

public class GitTest {
  public static void main(String[] args) {
    System.out.println("Git is fun");
  }
}
```

61.3. Creating a local Git repository

To put your new project under version control with Git, right-click on your project, select *Team →
Share Project → Git*.

Depending on your installation you may have to select that you want to use Git as a version control system.

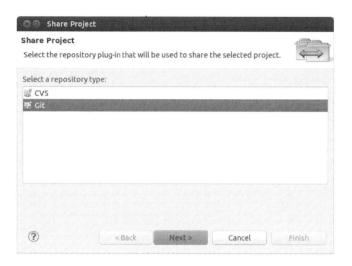

On the next dialog press the *Create* button.

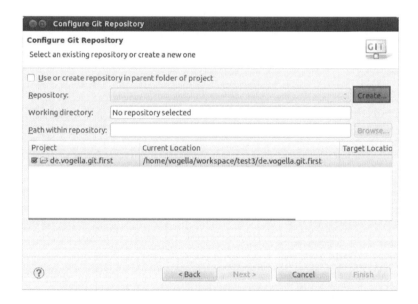

It is recommended to separate your Git repository from any additional meta-data which Eclipse might create, it is recommended to place your Git repositories outside the Eclipse workspace. Eclipse follows this recommendation and the EGit plug-in proposes a directory outside your workspace. Placing Git repositories directly in the workspace may cause performance issues since the Git support in Eclipse then may need to scan a large number of files reachable under the workspace.

Enter your project name as *Name* for your local Git repository. Select the *Finish* button.

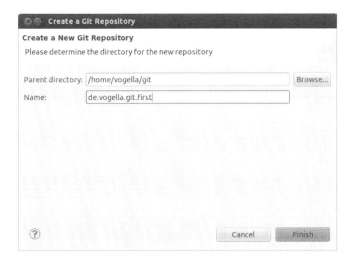

After pressing the *Finish* button, the wizard displays the settings for your local Git repository. Select the *Finish* button again to put your repository under Git version control.

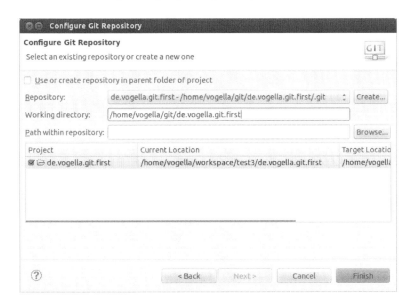

You have created a local Git repository. The Git repository is in this case directly stored in the specified folder in a .git folder. The following screenshot shows the generated directory structure.

```
vogella@angelus:~/git/de.vogella.git.first$ tree -a
├── de.vogella.git.first
│   ├── bin
│   │   └── de
│   │       └── vogella
│   │           └── git
│   │               └── first
│   │                   └── GitTest.class
│   ├── .classpath
│   ├── .project
│   ├── .settings
│   │   └── org.eclipse.jdt.core.prefs
│   ├── src
│   │   └── de
│   │       └── vogella
│   │           └── git
│   │               └── first
│   │                   └── GitTest.java
└── .git
    ├── branches
    ├── config
    ├── HEAD
    ├── hooks
    ├── logs
    │   └── refs
    │       └── heads
    ├── objects
    │   ├── info
    │   └── pack
    └── refs
        ├── heads
        └── tags
```

61.4. Create .gitignore file

Git can be configured to ignore certain files and directories. This is configured via the `.gitignore` file.

Create a `.gitignore` file in your Git repository with the following content.

```
bin
.metadata
```

All files and directories which apply to the pattern described in this file will be ignored by *Git*. In this example all files in the `bin` and the `.metadata` directory will be ignored.

You can also create a local `.gitignore` file by right-clicking on a resource (file or folder) and by selecting the *Team → Ignore* context menu entry. But excluding individual files should be avoided, you should prefer to define a pattern in your `.gitignore` file in the root directory of the repository.

Note

You can also configure Eclipse to automatically ignore derived resources, e.g. class files via the *Window → Preferences → Team → Git → Projects → Automatically ignore derived resources ..* setting.

61.5. Using the Git Staging view for the initial commit

Eclipse gives you several options to stage and commit your changes. The *Git Staging view* provides a convenient compact overview on all changes you have done since checking out a branch.

The *Git Staging view* is non-modal, you can switch between different repositories without loosing a commit message and it allows incremental staging for changes.

Open the *Git Staging view* via the *Window → Show View → Other... → Git → Git Staging* menu.

In this *view* select all files which have changed and drag them into the *Staged Changes* area. Write a descriptive commit message and press the *Commit* button which is hightlighted in the following screenshot.

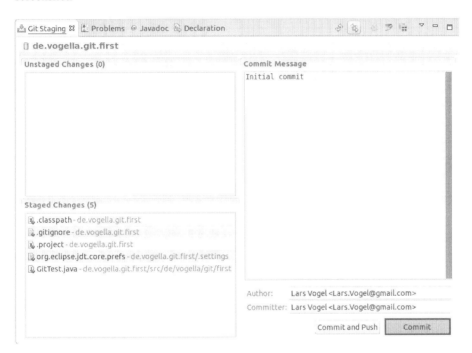

Afterwards the first version of your Java project is under version control. If you don't experience any hardware error your data is now savely stored in your local Git repository and you can always restore your Eclipse project to this initial point.

61.6. Using the Git Staging view for committing changes

Change the `System.out.println` message in your `GitTest` class.

```
package de.vogella.git.first;

public class GitTest {
```

```
public static void main(String[] args) {
    System.out.println("Git is cool");
  }
}
```

Also create a new file called readme.txt

We want to commit the changes of GitTest class but not add and commit the readme.txt file to the Git repository.

Using the *Git Staging view* drag only the GitTest class into the *Staged Changes* area, write a good commit message and press the commit button.

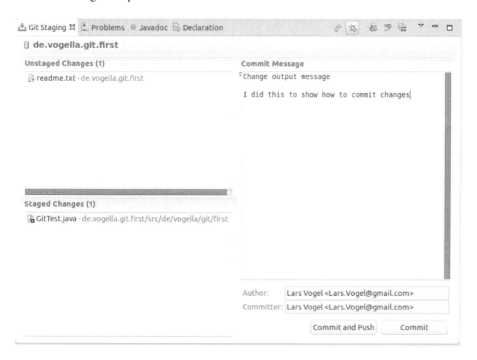

This change is now also stored in your local *Git* repository. The readme.txt is neither staged nor committed to the Git repository.

61.7. Staging and committing files in the Git commit dialog

The *Git Staging view* is a very convenient way of working with Git as it gives you a grouped view of all the pending changes without an additional dialog.

If you prefer to invoke the Git commit dialog directly you can do this via selecting the *Team → Commit* dialog.

The dialog allows you to add changed and new files to the staging area and commit the changes.

62

Analysing Git repositories with Eclipse

62.1. Package Explorer integration

The *Package Explorer view* shows indicators on the files to show their status. The most important icon decorators are depicted in the following screenshot.

▼ 📁 > gitfolder
    📄 added_to_index.txt
    📄 > dirty.txt
    📄 ignored.txt
    📄 staged.txt
    📄 tracked.txt
    📄 untracked.txt

The file name describes the state of the file from the following list:

• added to index - staged but not yet committed, i.e. snapshot of this file has been stored in the git database. This status is the same as the *staged* but the file wasn't under Git version control before

• dirty - file has changed since the last commit

• ignored - flagged to be ignored by Git

• staged - staged to be included in the next commit

• tracked - commit and not changed

• untracked - neither staged nor committed

 Note

Combination of the staged and dirty status means: some parts of the changed file have been staged while some are still unstaged. This can happen if you stage a file and then again modify the file before creating the next commit. You can also change the staged parts using the compare editor opened by double clicking files in the staging view.

On a project level the *Package Explorer view* adds to the label of the project name the information which Git repository is used. It also adds the number of commits that are different between local and remote tracking branch. This way you can quickly see if your local branch is ahead or behind the remote branch it is tracking.

▸ 🗄 com.example.e4.rcp.wizard.feature [eclipse4book master ↑2]

▸ 🗁 drag

▸ 🗄 > org.eclipse.e4.demo.contacts [eclipse.platform.ui master]

▸ 🗁 org.eclipse.e4.demo.contacts.feature

62.2. View the commit history

The *History view* allows you to analyze the commit timeline, see the branches, and to which commits they point, etc. This view is despited in the following screenshot.

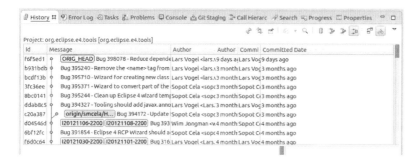

To see the history of a resource, select your project, a file or a folder, right-click on it and select the *Show in* → *History* context menu entry. Alternative you can use the Alt+Shift+W shortcut and select the *History* entry.

If you select a commit you see the commit message and the involved files.

Note

If you want to see more details about a commit, right-click it and select the *Open in Commit Viewer* entry.

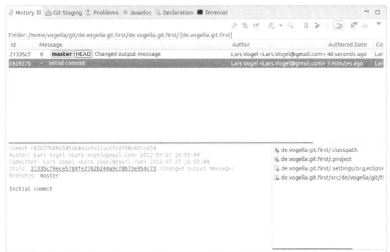

Via right-click on an individual file you can compare this file with its ancestor (the commit before that) or with the current version in the workspace.

The *History view* allows you to filter based on resources. See the tooltips of the toolbar for the meaning of the different filter options. In order to see all commits click the *Show all changes in this repository* and *Show all branches and tags* buttons.

Commits which are not reachable from any branch, tag or symbolic link, e.g. HEAD are not displayed in the *History view*.

You can also search for commits based on committer, author, ID or comment. The find feature of the history view is mainly interesting to quickly move to a commit you are searching.

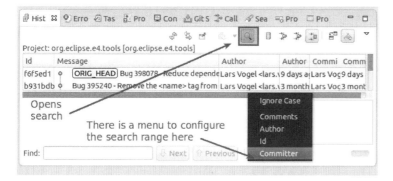

Note

The *Git Search* available in the *Search → Search* menu is much more powerful and consumes less memory since it doesn't need to also display the history.

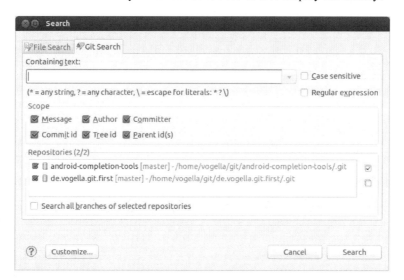

62.3. Repository view

62.3.1. Working with your Git repositories

EGit has a *Git repository view* which allow you to browse your repositories, clone Git repositories, checkout projects, manage your branches and much more.

The toolbar entries allow you to add an existing local Git repository to the view, clone a Git repository and to create a new Git repository.

Create a new
Git repo

Clone existing
Git repo

Add local Git repo

62.3.2. Content area

The content area show the existing Git repositories and the structural elements of this view. The following screenshot highlights the different main elements of this *view*.

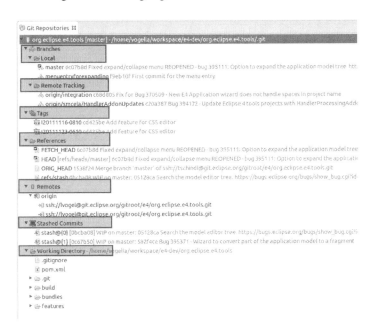

A right-click (context menu) on an element in the *Git repository view* allows you to perform related Git operations. For example if you click on a branch you can checkout the branch or delete it.

62.3.3. Open a commit

If you are in the *Git repository view* you can open a commit via *Navigate* → *Open Git Commit* menu entry.

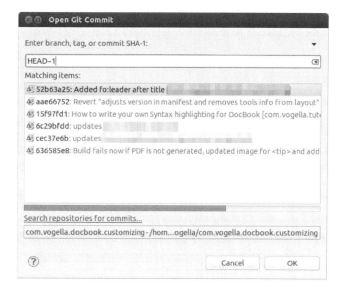

62.3.4. Possible operations from a commit

If you open a commit you can create a tag or branch from it. You can also revert it, cherry pick it or check it out.

63

Cloning Git repositories and importing projects

63.1. Clone existing project

Eclipse allows you to clone an existing Git repository and to import existing projects from this repository into your Eclipse workspace by using a wizard.

Select *File → Import → Git → Project from Git*.

Select *URI* in the next dialog.

Enter the URL to your Git repository. Git supports several protocols, e.g. $git://$ and $https://$. You only have to paste the URL to the first line of the dialog, the rest will be filled out automatically.

Please note that some proxy servers block the $git://$ protocol. If you face issues, please try to use the $https://$ or $http://$ protocol.

For example the following URI can be used to clone the example projects of the Eclipse 4 application development book: git://github.com/vogella/eclipse4book.git

The above links uses the git protocol, alternatively you can also use the http protocol: http://github.com/vogella/eclipse4book.git

After pressing the *Next* button the system will allow you to import the existing branches. You should select at least *master* as this is typically the main development branch.

The next dialog allows you to specify where the project should be copied to and which branch should be initially selected.

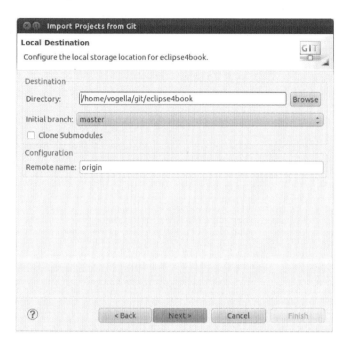

After the Git repository is cloned, *EGit* opens an additional import dialog which allows to import the Eclipse projects from the Git repository.

Once this dialog is completed, you have checked out (cloned) the projects into a local Git repository and you can use Git operation on these projects.

63.2. Import projects from existing repository

If you have already an existing Git repository you can import existing Eclipse projects into your workspace via the *File → Import* menu entry.

Select *File → Import → Git → Project from Git*.

Select *Local* in the next dialog and enter the path to the Git repository. The wizard allows you to import existing projects. After this import Eclipse makes the projects available and is aware that these projects are part of a Git repository.

64

Common Git operations in Eclipse

64.1. Performing Git operations in Eclipse

64.1.1. Basic operations

Once you have placed a project under version control you can start using team operations on your project. The team operations are available via right-click on your project or file.

The most important operations are described in the following list. Select:

- *Team → Add to index*, to add the selected resource(s) to the index of Git

- *Team → Commit*, to open the commit dialog for committing to your Git repository

- *Team → Create Patch...*, to create a patch

- *Team → Apply Patch...*, to apply a patch to your file system

- *Team → Ignore*, to add the file to a .gitignore file

- *Team → Show in History*, to display the selected files and folders in the *History view*

If you select a project you can use additional team operations from the context menu.

- *Team → Pull* to pull in changes from your remote Git repository

- *Team → Fetch* to fetch the current state from the remote repository

- *Team → Switch To* to switch or create new branches

- *Team → Push* to push changes to your remote Git repository

- *Team → Tag* to create and manage tags.

64.1.2. Commit amend

Git amend allows to adjust the last commit. For example you can change the commit message. The *Git Staging view* allows you to perform the Git amend command via the highlighted button in the following screenshot.

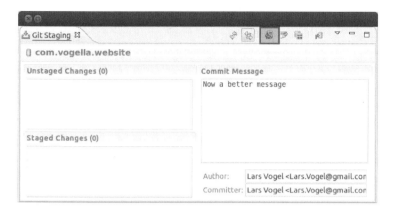

64.2. Using compare and replace

64.2.1. Comparing files

Eclipse allows you to compare a selected file with another commit or with the Git index. The selection is depicted in the following screenshot.

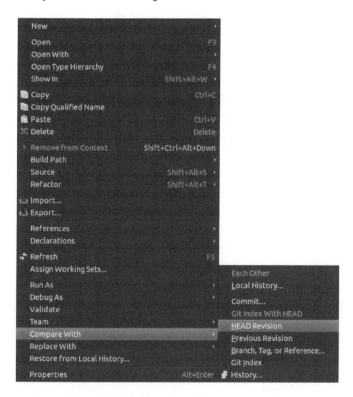

64.2.2. Replace files

Similar to compare the *Team → Replace with* allows you to replace the current selection with a commit or the Git index.

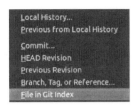

65

Branching with Eclipse

65.1. What are branches?

Git allows you to create *branches*, i.e. named pointers to commits. You can work on different branches independently from each other. The default branch is called *master*.

Git allows you to create branches very fast and cheaply in terms of resource consumption. Developers are encouraged to use local branches frequently.

If you decide to work on a branch, you *checkout* this branch. This means that Git moves the *HEAD* pointer to the new branch which points to a commit and populates the *working tree* with the content of this commit.

Untracked files remain unchanged and are available in the new branch. This allows you to create a branch for unstaged and uncommited changes at any point in time.

Also dirty files remain unchanged and stay dirty. If Git would need to modify a dirty file on checkout, the checkout fails with a "checkout conflict" error. This prevent that you loose any changes. The changes must in this case committed, reverted or stashed.

65.2. Branching in Eclipse

Right-click your project and select *Team → Branch* to create new branches or to switch between existing branches. You can also switch branches in the *History view*.

66

Resetting your Branch

66.1. git reset to move the HEAD pointer

The `git reset` command allows you to set the current HEAD to a specified state, e.g. commit. This way you can continue your work from another commit.

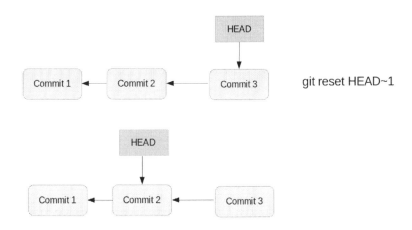

Via certain parameters you can define how the index and the working tree is updated. These parameters are listed in the following table.

Table 66.1. git reset

Reset	Working tree	Index
soft	No	No
mixed (default)	No	Yes
hard	Yes	Yes

The `git reset` command does not remove files that are not staged nor committed.

66.2. Resetting in Eclipse

The *History view* allows you to reset your current branch to a commit. Right-click on a certain commit and select *Reset* and the reset mode you would like to use.

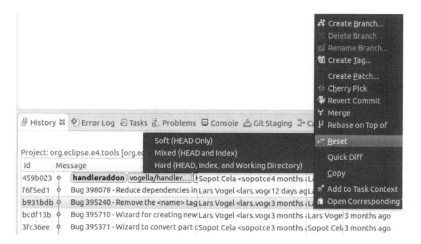

The *Git Reflog view* keeps track of the movements of the HEAD pointer. This *view* allows you to find commit again, e.g. if you used the `git reset --hard` command to remove certain commits.

Merging in Eclipse

67.1. Merging

Git allows you to combine the changes of two branches. This process is called *merging*.

67.2. Fast-forward merge

If the commits which are merged are direct successors of the *HEAD* pointer of the current branch, Git simplifies things by performing a so-called *fast forward merge*. This *fast forward merge* simply moves the *HEAD* pointer of the current branch to the last commit which is being merged.

This process is depicted in the following graphics. The first picture assumes that master is checked out and that you want to merge the changes of the branch labeled "branch" into your "master" branch. Each commit points to its successor.

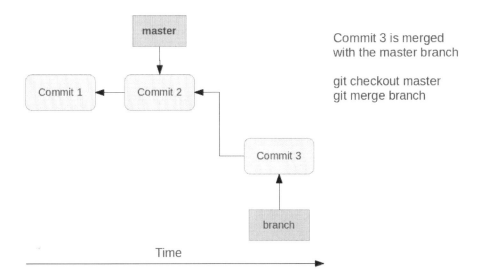

After the fast forward merge the *HEAD* pointer of "master" now points to the existing commit.

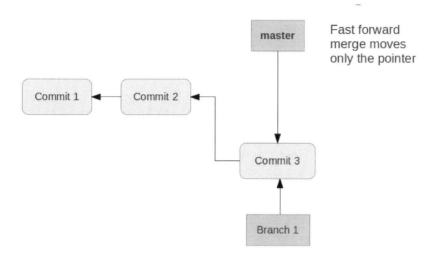

Fast forward
merge moves
only the pointer

67.3. Merge commit

If commits are merged which are not direct successors of the *HEAD* pointer of the current branch, Git performs a so-called *three-way-merge* between the latest snapshot of two branches, based on the most recent common ancestor of both.

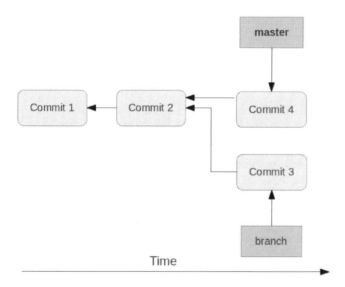

As a result a so-called *merge commit* is created on the current branch which is combining the respective changes from the two branches being merged. This commit points to both its predecessors.

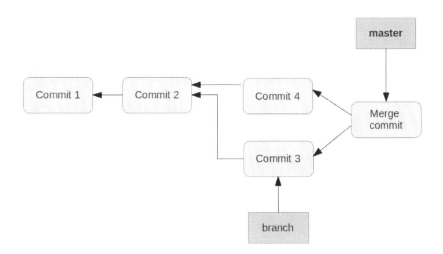

67.4. Merge

EGit supports merging of branches to add the changes of one branch into another. Select your project and *Team → Merge* to start the merge dialog.

67.5. Solving merge conflicts

If you pull in changes or merge a branch and you have conflicting changes, EGit will highlight the affected files. EGit also supports the resolution of these merge conflicts.

Right-click on a file with merge conflicts and select *Team → Merge Tool*.

Tip

Use the *Git staging view* to find the conflicting files, in large projects that is usually faster than navigating the *Package Explorer view*.

This opens a dialog, asking you which merge mode you would like to use. The easiest way to see the conflicting changes is to use the *Use HEAD (the last local version) of conflicting files* as merge mode. This way you see the original changes on the left side and the conflicting changes on the right side.

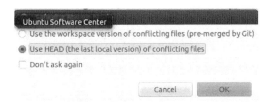

You can manually edit the text on the left side or use the *Copy current change from right to left* button to copy the conflicting changes from right to left.

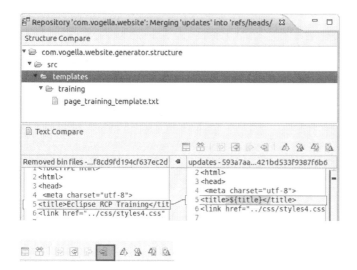

Once you have manually merged the changes, select *Team → Add* from the context menu of the resource to mark the conflicts as resolved and commit the merge resolution via *Team → Commit*.

68

Other Git operations with Eclipse

68.1. Create patches

A patch is a text file which contains instructions how to update a set of files to a different state.

If you use Git you can create a patch for the changes you made. This patch can be applied to the file system.

To create a patch for a set of changes with EGit, select the resources for which you want to create a patch in the *Package Explorer view*, right click and select *Team → Create Patch*.

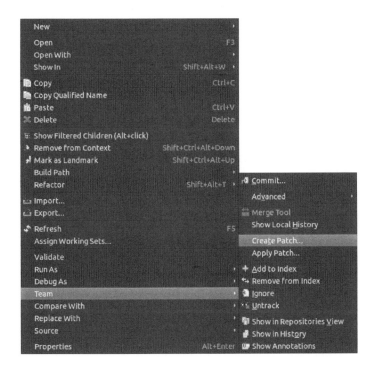

The resulting file can be used to get applied to another Git repository, via *Team → Apply Patch*.

68.2. Blame annotations

EGit allows to add annotations to see which line was last changed by whom and which commit. To enable this, right-click on your file and select *Team → Show Annotations*.

Afterwards you can place the mouse on the left side of the editor and a popup will show the commit information.

68.3. The stash command

Git provides the `git stash` command which allows you to save the current uncommitted changes and checkout the last committed revision.

This allows you to pull in the latest changes or to develop an urgent fix. Afterwards you can restore the stashed changes, which will reapply the changes to the current version of the source code.

In general using the stash command should be the exception in using Git. Typically you would create new branches for new features and switch between branches. You can also commit frequently in your local Git repository and use interactive rebase to combine these commits later before pushing them to another Git repository.

You can also avoid using `git stash` if you commit the changes you want to put aside and use the `git commit --amend` to change the commit later. In this you typically put a marker in the commit message to mark it as a draft, e.g. "[DRAFT] implement feature x".

68.4. Stash via the Git repository view

The `git stash` command is available in the *Git repositories view*. Right-click on your Git repository and select *Stash Changes*.

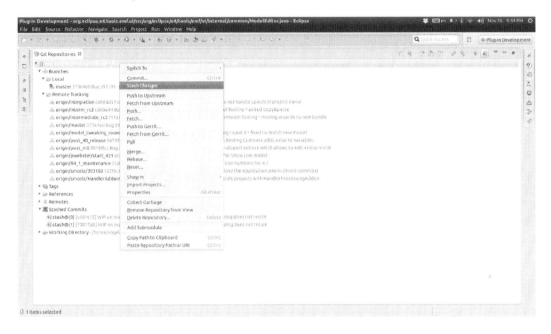

69

Multi projects in one Git repository

69.1. Git repository for multiple projects

69.1.1. Create a new repository

Eclipse allows to work with projects that are not included in the workspace.

To put several Eclipse projects into the same Git repository you can create a folder inside or outside your workspace and create the projects inside this folder. Then create a Git repository for this folder and all projects in this folder will be handled by the same repository. The best practice is to put the Git repository outsite of the Eclipse workspace.

You can import these projects into your workspace via *File → Import → Git → Projects from Git* as explained before.

69.1.2. Add a project to an existing Git repository

To add a new Eclipse project to an existing Git repository, select the project, right-click on it and select *Team → Share → Git* and select the existing Git repository.

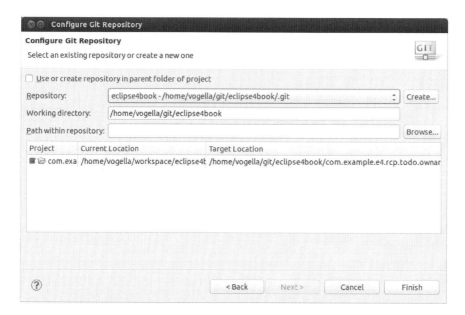

EGit moves the projects to the repository and imports the project automatically into your workspace.

69.2. Tutorial: Create Git repository for multiple projects

Create two Java projects called *com.vogella.egit.multi.java1* and *com.vogella.egit.multi.java2*.

Create at least one Java class in each project.

Note

Git doesn't track the history of empty folders, it is tracking file content and content changes.

Afterwards select both projects, right-click on them and select *Team → Share Project... → Git*. Eclipse may ask you which version control system you want to use, e.g. *CVS* or *Git*. Select, of course, the Git entry.

Now create a new Git repository outside your workspace similar to the process you used for the creation of your first Git repository in the book.

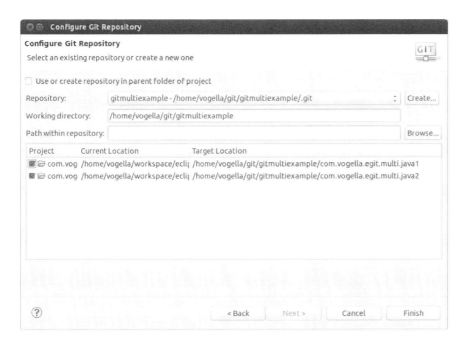

You created a new Git repository which contains both projects. Both projects are moved to this new repository.

Now perform your initial commit for all files in the projects to store the file in the new Git repository.

70

Working with Github

70.1. Github

Github is a popular hosting provider for Git projects and if your repository is a *public* repository the hosting at Github is free. A *public* repository is visible to everyone and can be cloned by other people at any point in time.

To use GitHub create an account on the Github Website [https://github.com/].

Github allows you to use the authentication via password or via SSH key to access your repositories.

70.2. Create repository in Github

Create a new repository on Github for example *de.vogella.git.github*.

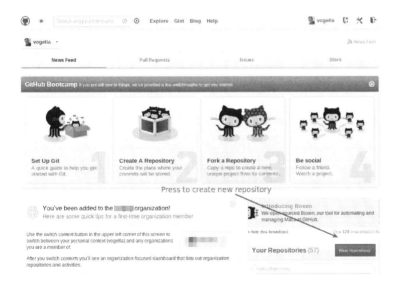

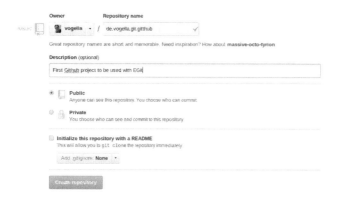

After creation of your new repository Github displays the information what you have to do if you want to connect to this repository via the command line. As we are going to use EGit you can ignore this information.

70.3. Clone project

Copy the URL from Github and select in Eclipse from the menu the *File → Import → Git → Projects from Git*

Eclipse fills out most of the fields based on the URL in the clipboard. Enter your user and password to be able to push to Github. Alternative you can also use an SSH key. You can configure Eclipse to know your SSH via the *Window → Preferences → General → Network Connection → SSH2* preference setting. This setting is depicted in the following screenshot.

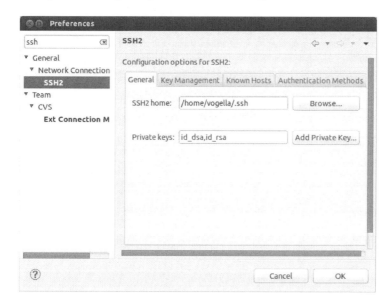

70.4. Push changes

After you made changes and committed them to your local repository, you can select *Team → Push to upstream* on the project folder, to push your changes to your Github. This requires write access to the Github repository.

70.5. Mylyn integration with Github

Eclipse Mylyn provides task integration for Github issues, Github pull and Gist (short text snippets) into the Eclipse IDE.

There is a GitHub connector for Mylyn available, please see Github Mylyn User Guide [http:// wiki.eclipse.org/EGit/GitHub/UserGuide] for details.

You install it via *Help → Install new Software* and the update site of your release.

Now you can integrate your Github issues into Eclipse via *File → Import... → Task → GitHub Task Repositories* and by following the wizard.

You can also import now directly projects from Github repositories.

For a detailed description of the Mylyn and EGit integration please see the following webpage.

```
http://wiki.eclipse.org/EGit/GitHub/UserGuide
```

Part XV. Introduction to
Eclipse plug-in development

71

Extending the Eclipse IDE

One of the advantages of using the Eclipse IDE is that the IDE can be extended by every developer. The developer can contribute new software components (plug-ins) for the Eclipse IDE. He even can offer own extension points which can be extended again by other developers.

This chapter gives an introduction intro the development of Eclipse *plug-ins*. This chapter is only an introduction to this topic as a complete introduction for Eclipse Plug-in development would fill another book.

71.1. Developing Eclipse plug-ins

A software component in Eclipse is called a *plug-in*.

The Eclipse IDE allows the developer to extend the IDE functionality via plug-ins. For example you can create new menu entries and associated actions via plug-ins.

71.2. Eclipse extensions and extension points

Eclipse provides the concept of *extension points* and *extensions* to allow functionality to be contributed to plug-ins by several other plug-ins.

Extensions and Extension points are defined via the `plugin.xml` file.

The following table describes the terminology.

Table 71.1. Extensions and extension points table

Term	Description
Plug-in defines extension point	Allows other plug-ins to add functionality based on the contract defined by the extension point. The plug-in which defines the extension point is also responsible for evaluating the extensions. Therefore the defining plug-in typically contains coding to evaluate the extensions.
A plug-in provides an extension	This plug-in provides an extension (contribution) based on the contract defined by an existing extension point. Contributions can be code or data.

The Eclipse plug-in development environment (PDE) provides a structured editor for the `plugin.xml` file. If you have the PDE tooling installed, you can open this editor via a double-click on the `plugin.xml` file. Select the *Extensions* tab to define *extensions* which are contributed by your plug-in. Select the *Extension Points* tab to see the *extension points* which your plug-in defines.

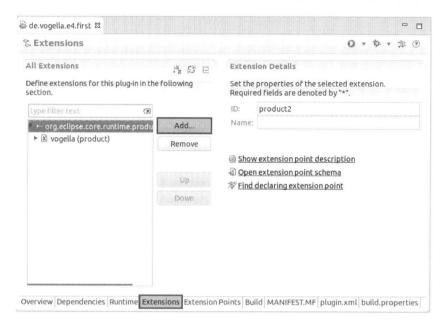

Using the *Add* button you can add new *extensions*. Once you added an *extension* you typically right-click on its elements to add elements or attributes to the *extensions*.

Typically Eclipse plug-in developers contribute more *extensions* to existing *extension points* than writing new *extension points*.

72

Installation

72.1. Downloading or upgrading

To get the required Eclipse tooling for plug-in development you have two options. You can download a special version of Eclipse to develop plug-ins or your can upgrade an existing Eclipse Java IDE.

Both approaches require that you have Java already installed.

72.2. Download the Eclipse plug-in package

Browse to the Eclipse download site [http://www.eclipse.org/downloads] and download the *Eclipse Classic* package.

Extract the downloaded file to your harddisk. Avoid having special characters or spaces in the path to your extract Eclipse.

72.3. Update an Eclipse Java IDE

In case you have downloaded the Eclipse Java IDE (or any other non RCP flavor) distribution you can use the Eclipse *update manager* to install the plug-ins required for RCP development.

To open the update manager select *Help → Install new Software....*

Install *General Purpose Tools → Eclipse Plug-in Development Environment → Eclipse RCP Plug-in Developer Resources* from the Eclipse update site for your release. This would be for example http://

download.eclipse.org/releases/kepler for the Eclipse 4.3. release. You may have to remove the *Group items by category* flag to see all available features.

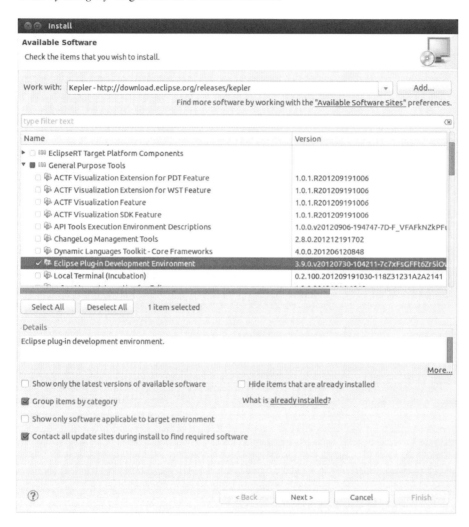

73

Tutorial: Developing a simple plug-in

73.1. Create project

We will create a plug-in which contributes a menu entry to the standard Eclipse menu.

Create a new plug-in project called `com.vogella.plugin.first` via *File → New → Project → Plug-in Development → Plug-in Project*.

Enter the data as depicted in the following screenshots.

Select the *Hello, World Command!* template and press the *Next* button.

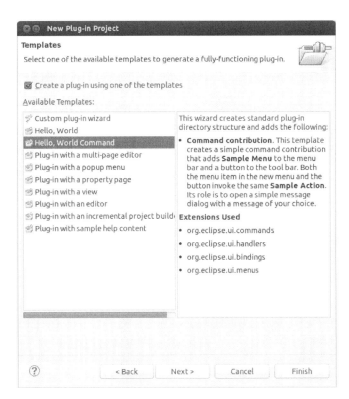

The last page of the wizard allows you to customize the values of the wizard. You can leave the default values and press the *Finish* button.

Eclipse may ask you if you want to switch to the plug-in development perspective. Answer *Yes* if you are prompted.

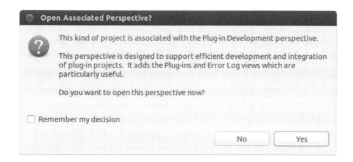

As result the following project is created.

73.2. Start an Eclipse IDE with your plug-in

Eclipse allows you to start a new Eclipse IDE with your plug-in included.

For this, select either your project folder or your MANIFEST.MF file, right-click on it and select *Run-As → Eclipse Application*.

A new Eclipse workbench starts. This runtime Eclipse has your new menu entry included. If you select this menu entry a message box will be displayed.

74

More on Eclipse plug-in development

74.1. Plug-in development extended

The previous chapter could only touch the starting points of extending the Eclipse IDE. vogella.com provides an extensive list of online tutorials to extend the Eclipse IDE.

74.2. Webressources

Please see vogella Eclipse plug-in tutorials [http://www.vogella.com/eclipse.html] and Eclipse resources [http://www.eclipse.org/resources/] for a list of online Eclipse plug-in development tutorials.

74.3. Building Eclipse RCP applications

It is possible to run the Eclipse programming model to create native stand-alone applications called Eclipse RCP applications.

An Eclipse 4 RCP application typically uses the base components of the Eclipse platform and adds additional application specific components.

The author of this book has published the *Eclipse 4 RCP* book which covers the creation of Eclipse RCP applications. You find more about the books published by vogella under vogella books [http://www.vogella.com/books.html].

75

Deploy your software component (plug-ins) locally

75.1. Options for installation

You have several options to make your plug-in available in your Eclipse IDE. You can:

- Install your plug-in directly into your Eclipse installation from your Eclipse IDE

- Export your plug-in and copy it into your Eclipse installation into the `dropins` folder

- Create a update site and use the Eclipse update manager to install it from this site

The following describes all approaches.

75.2. Installing your plug-in from your Eclipse IDE

You can install your plug-in directly into your running Eclipse IDE.

The Eclipse plug-in export wizard has an option for this. Open the export wizard via *File → Export → Plug-in Development → Deployable plug-ins and fragments.*

In the export wizard dialog select in this case *Install into host. Repository*. This is depicted in the following screenshot.

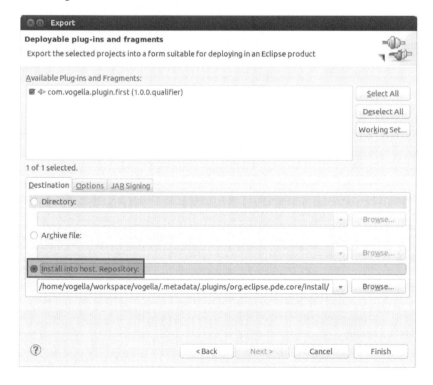

75.3. Export plug-in and put into dropins folder

If you export your plug-in locally you can put it into the Eclipse `dropins` folder of your Eclipse installation. After a restart of your Eclipse your plug-in should be available and ready for use.

Open again the export wizard via *File → Export → Plug-in Development → Deployable plug-ins and fragments*.

Select the plug-in you want to export and the folder to which this plug-in should get exported.

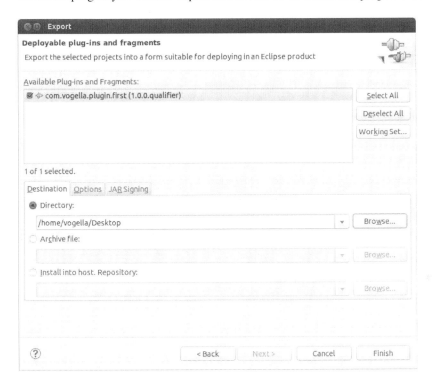

Press the *Finish* button. This creates a `jar` file with the exported plug-in in the selected directory.

Copy this jar to the `dropins` directory in your Eclipse installation directory and re-start Eclipse.

After a restart of Eclipse your plug-in is available in your Eclipse installation and ready to be used.

76

Create update site

76.1. Creating update sites

You can also create an update site for your plug-in. An update site consists of static files which can be placed on a fileserver or a webserver. Other users can install Eclipse plug-in from this update site.

This requires that you create a feature project for the plug-in. You can export this feature project and use the Eclipse update manager to install the feature (with the plug-in).

You also need a category as the Eclipse update manager shows by default only features with a category. While the user can de-select this grouping you should always include a category for your exported feature to make it easy for the user to install your feature.

76.2. Create feature project

Create a feature project for your plug-in and add your plug-in to this feature. You create a feature project via *File → New → Other... → Plug-in Development → Feature Project*.

Create the feature project similar to the following screenshots.

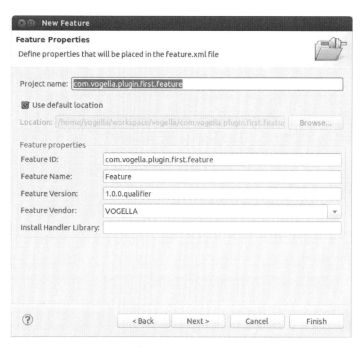

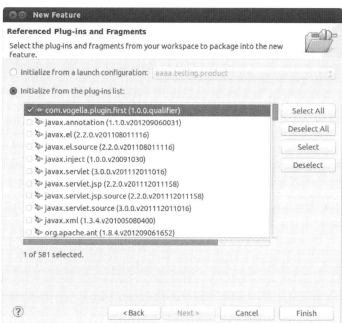

76.3. Create category definition

In your feature project create via the menu entry *File → New → Other... → Plug-in development →
Category Definition* a new category definition.

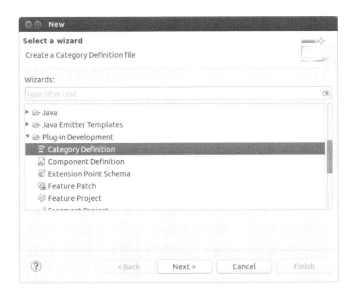

Press the *New Category* button and create a category with a name which describes your functionality.
Add your feature to this category.

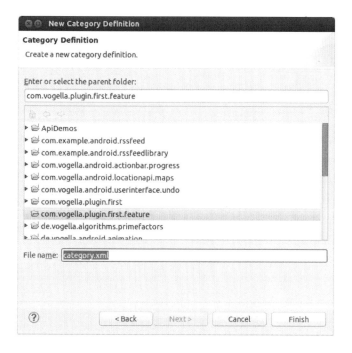

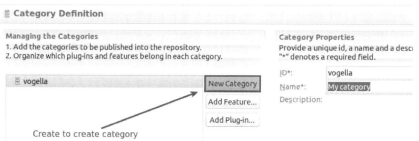

76.4. Create an update site

You can create an update site for your feature in a local directory on your machine. For this, select *File* → *Export* → *Deployable features*.

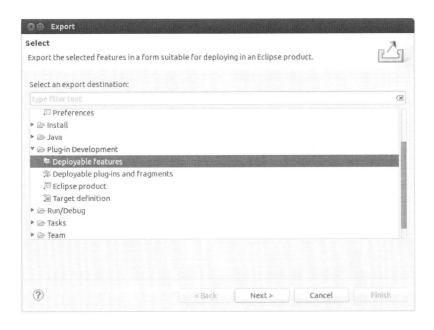

To use your category, switch to the *Options* tab and select the path to your `category.xml` file in the *Categorize repository* option.

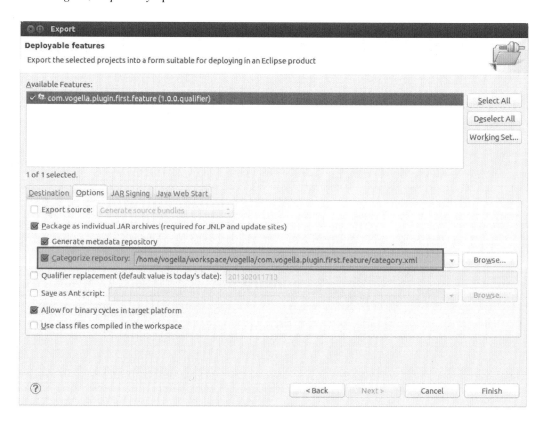

76.5. Install feature via the Eclipse update manager

Use the Eclipse update manager via *Help → Install new software* to install this new feature into your Eclipse IDE.

Use the update manager and point to your local directory and select and install your feature. In case you don't see your feature, try deselecting the *Group items by category* flag. In this case you have forgotten to use your category during the export.

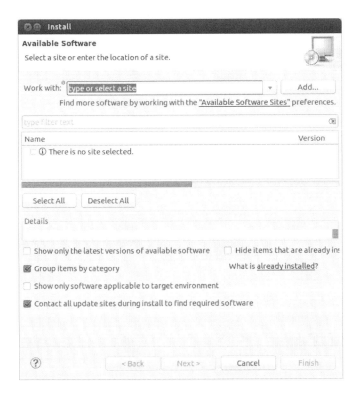

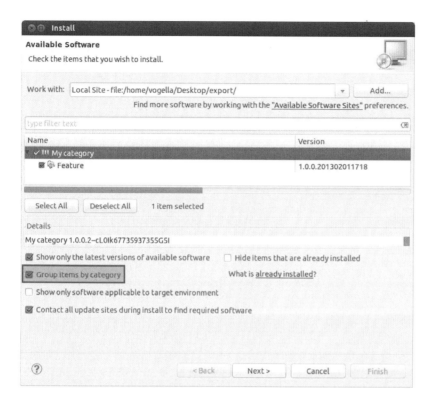

Restart the Eclipse IDE after the installation. After a restart of Eclipse your plug-in should now be available in your Eclipse installation and ready to be used.

76.6. Exercise: Deploy and install your plug-in via update site

Create a feature project for your `com.vogella.plugin.first` plug-in and export it as Eclipse update site.

Use the Eclipse update manager to install the new feature into your Eclipse IDE.

77

Eclipse IDE development build and custom build

77.1. Download and install Eclipse development build

The Eclipse project has a simultaneous release every year at the end of June. In June 2012 the official release was Eclipse 4.2, by June 2013 Eclipse 4.3 is released.

The Eclipse project creates regular builds of the next releases. You find *Stable Builds* which are tested by the community. These milestone (M) and release candidate (RC) builds are created based on a predefined time schedule.

Integration, *Nightly* and *Maintenance* builds are test builds which are automatically created and which do not receive additional manual testing. But if they produced after the stable builds, they contain the same fixes as the stable builds.

In general milestone and RC builds are relative stable compared to integration builds but may not contain the latest features and patches.

You find the builds for the next Eclipse release (currently Eclipse 4.3) under the following URL: Eclipse download page [http://download.eclipse.org/eclipse/downloads/]

77.2. Creating a custom Eclipse build

Eclipse provides a Maven based build system which allows you to build the Eclipse IDE locally. The Eclipse projects uses the Git version control system, which allows you to change the source code of Eclipse and commit these changes locally to your own Git repository.

Currently the setup of the Eclipse build is still under development. If you want to build the Eclipse IDE yourself you can check the following webpage for detailed build instructions. See Eclipse Platform Build [http://wiki.eclipse.org/Platform-releng/Platform_Build] for details.

Part XVI. Additional Eclipse resources

78

Eclipse online resources

This chapter lists resources with further information about Eclipse.

78.1. Online documentations

The Eclipse help system is available from within your Eclipse installation as well as online.

With your running Eclipse IDE you can access the online help via *Help → Help Contents*. This will start a new window which shows you the help topics for your currently installed components.

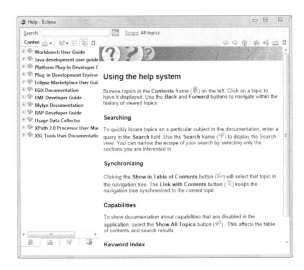

Online you find the online help under the following link: Eclipse online help [http://help.eclipse.org]. The online help is version dependent and contains the help for all Eclipse projects included in the selected release. The above link points to the online help of the current release.

78.2. Webresources

The Eclipse homepage also contains a list of relevant resources about Eclipse and Eclipse programming. You find these resources under the following link: Eclipse resources [http://www.eclipse.org/resources/].

You also find several tutorials about the Eclipse IDE on the following webpage: vogella Eclipse IDE tutorials [http://www.vogella.com/eclipse.html].

79

Eclipse Bug reporting and questions

79.1. Asking (and answering) questions

Due to the complexity and extensibility of Eclipse you will need additional resources to help you resolve your specific problems. Fortunately the web contains several resources which can help you with your Eclipse problems.

Currently the best places to ask questions are the Eclipse forums [http://eclipse.org/forums] and Stack Overflow [http://stackoverflow.com].

The *Eclipse forums* offer several topic specific forums in which you can post and answer questions. To post questions in the Eclipse forums you need a valid user account in the Eclipse bug tracker. The advantage of the Eclipse forums is that, depending on the topic, developers of Eclipse projects (*Eclipse committers*) are also active there and might directly answer your question.

Stack Overflow also requires a user account and its community is also very active. *Stack Overflow* does not have separate forums for specific questions. In *Stack Overflow* you tag your questions with the relevant keyword, e.g. *Eclipse* and people search for them or subscribe to them.

Both places are excellent places to ask questions. If you ask a question it is in general good advice to be polite and to give a good error description as this motivates people to give you high quality answers.

Note

Ensure that you search the forums and mailing lists for solutions for your problem since often somebody else already asked the same question earlier and the answer is already available.

79.2. Eclipse Bugs

Eclipse has a public bug tracker based on *Bugzilla*. *Mozilla Bugzilla* is an Open Source project.

This bugtracker can be found under https://bugs.eclipse.org/bugs/. Here you can search for existing bugs and review them.

To participate actively in the Eclipse bugtracker you need to create a new account. This can be done by pressing the *Open a New Account* link.

Once you have a user account, you can login to the Eclipse bug tracker. This allows you to comment on existing bugs and report new ones.

Note

The user for the Eclipse forum and the bug tracker is the same.

80
Closing words

I hope you enjoyed your learning experience with the Eclipse IDE. The Eclipse platform is created by an active community of developers. You find frameworks and tooling for most use cases, reaching from Python and PHP development to mobile developer for Android.

In case you are missing a certain functionality most likely a commercial or Open Source project exists which provides the desired functionality. This is really unique for an IDE.

Eclipse also allows you to easily extend the Eclipse IDE or even to create Eclipse based applications. Eclipse is also under active development. Please use the Eclipse Forum or the Eclipse bug tracker to provide feedback and bug reports.

I have personally never regretted to select the Eclipse IDE as my primary IDE. Eclipse is flexible, extendible and has a helpful and active community. I hope you continue to enjoy the usage of Eclipse.

Lars Vogel

Appendix A. Shortcuts

The following description gives an overview of the most important shortcuts for Eclipse.

A.1. Shortcuts

A.1.1. Using shortcuts in Eclipse

Using shortcuts make a developer more productive. Eclipse provides keyboard shortcuts for the most common actions. Using shortcuts is usually preferable as you can perform actions much faster.

Eclipse supports of course the typical shortcuts, e.g. **Ctrl+S** for saving, **Ctrl+C** for copying the selected text or file and **Ctrl+V** for pasting the element currently in the clipboard.

A.1.2. Shortcuts on Mac OS

This description uses the shortcuts based on Windows and Linux. Mac OS uses the Cmd key frequently instead of the Ctrl key.

A.2. Quick Access

The Ctrl+3 shortcut allows you to perform all available actions in Eclipse. This shortcut puts the focus into the *Quick Access* search box which allows you to execute any Eclipse command.

For example you can open a *Preference*, a *Wizard*, a *view* and a *Preference* page.

You can also use *Quick Access* to search for an opened editor by typing in the name of the resource which the editor shows.

The following screenshot shows how you could use Ctrl+3 to open the *Wizard* to create a new Java class.

A.3. Navigation

A.3.1. Globally available navigation shortcuts

Eclipse provides shortcuts for opening files or Java artifacts.

Table A.1. Navigation

Shortcut	Description
Ctrl + Shift + R	Search dialog for resources, e.g. text files

Shortcut	Description
Ctrl + Shift + T	Search dialog for Java Types
Ctrl + E	Search dialog to select an editor from the currently open editors
Ctrl + F8	Shortcut for switching perspectives

A.3.2. Navigation shortcuts in the editor

If you are working in the Java editor you can also use certain shortcuts for faster navigation. The following tables lists a few of them.

Table A.2. Search from an editor

Shortcut	Description
F3	Opens editor to selected element (type) or navigate to the declaration of the selected variable
Ctrl + .	Go to the next problem / error
Ctrl + ,	Go to the previous problem / error
F4 on a variable	Show type hierarchy
Ctrl + J	Incremental search without popup dialog, just starting typing to search. Press Ctrl + J to find the next match
Ctrl + K	Searches the selected text or if nothing is selected the last search from the *Find* dialog.
Ctrl + Shift + G	In the Java editor, s\earch for references in the workspace
Ctrl + Shift + P	Select the matching bracket. Cursor needs to be placed before or after a bracket.

Table A.3. Navigation between editors

Shortcut	Description
Alt + ←	Go to previous opened editor. Cursor is placed where it was before you opened the next editor
Alt + →	Similar Alt + ← but opens the next editor
Ctrl + Q	Go to editor and the position in this editor where the last edit was done
Ctrl + PageUp	Switch to previous opened editor
Ctrl + PageDown	Switch to next opened editor

A.4. Start Java programs

Table A.4. Running programs

Shortcut	Description
Ctrl + F11	Run last launched

Shortcut	Description
Alt + Shift + X, J	Run current selected class as Java application

A.5. Editing

The following lists contains useful keyboard shortcuts if you are inside your Java editor.

Table A.5. Handling the editor

Shortcut	Description
Ctrl + 1	Quickfix; result depending on cursor position
Ctrl + Space	Content assist/ code completion
Ctrl + T	Show the inheritance tree of the current Java class or method.
Ctrl + O	Show all methods of the current class, press Ctrl + O again to show the inherited methods.
Ctrl + M	Maximize active editor or view
Ctrl + Shift + F	Format source code
Ctrl + I	Correct indentation, e.g. format tabs/whitespaces in code
Ctrl + F	Opens the find dialog
Ctrl + Shift + O	Organize the imports; adds missing import statements and removes unused ones
Ctrl + Alt + Z	Wrap the select block of code into a block, e.g. try/catch.

Table A.6. Cursor navigation and text selection

Shortcut	Description
Ctrl + $\leftarrow$ or Ctrl + $\rightarrow$	Move one text element in the editor to the left or right
Ctrl + $\uparrow$ or $\downarrow$	Scroll up / down a line in the editor
Ctrl + Shift + P	Go to the matching bracket
Shift + Cursor movement	Select text from the starting position of the cursor
Alt + Shift $\uparrow$ / $\downarrow$	Select the previous / next syntactical element
Alt + Shift $\uparrow$ / $\downarrow$ / $\leftarrow$ / $\rightarrow$	Extending / reducing the selection of the previous / next syntactical element

Table A.7. Copy and move lines

Shortcut	Description
Ctrl + Alt + Cusor Down	Copy current line below the line in which the cursor is placed
Ctrl + Alt + Cusor Up	Copy current line above the line in which the cursor is placed
Alt + Up	Move line one line up
Alt + Down	Move line one line down

Table A.8. Delete

Shortcut	Description
Ctrl + D	Deletes line
Ctrl + Shift + DEL	Delete until end of line
Ctrl + DEL	Delete next element
Ctrl + BACKSPACE	Delete previous element

Table A.9. Create new lines

Shortcut	Description
Shift + Enter	Adds a blank line below the current line and moves the cursor to the new line. The difference between a regular enter is that the currently line is unchanged, independently of the position of the cursor.
Ctrl+Shift+Enter	Same as Shift + Enter but above

Table A.10. Variable assignment

Shortcut	Description
Ctrl + 2, L	Assign statement to new local variable
Ctrl + 2, F	Assign statement to new field

A.6. Coding

Table A.11. Coding

Shortcut	Description
Shift + F2	Show the Javadoc for the selected type / class / method
Alt+Shift + N	Shortcut for the menu to create new objects
Alt + Shift + Z	Surround block with try and catch

A.7. Refactoring

Table A.12. Refactoring

Shortcut	Description
Alt + Shift + R	Rename
Ctrl + 2, R	Rename locally (in file), faster than Alt + Shift + R
Alt + Shift + T	Opens the context-sensitive refactoring menu, e.g. displays

Index

Symbols

2419249R00220

Printed in Germany
by Amazon Distribution
GmbH, Leipzig